Rethinking Grading

Another ASCD book by Cathy Vatterott:

Rethinking Homework: Best Practices That Support Diverse Needs

ASCD MEMBER BOOK

Many ASCD members received this book as a
member benefit upon its initial release.

Learn more at: **www.ascd.org/memberbooks**

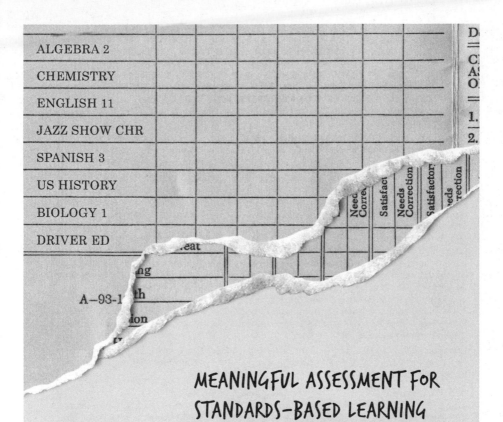

ALGEBRA 2

CHEMISTRY

ENGLISH 11

JAZZ SHOW CHR

SPANISH 3

US HISTORY

BIOLOGY 1

DRIVER ED

MEANINGFUL ASSESSMENT FOR
STANDARDS-BASED LEARNING

Rethinking Grading

Cathy Vatterott

ASCD | Alexandria, VA USA

1703 N. Beauregard St. • Alexandria, VA 22311-1714 USA
Phone: 800-933-2723 or 703-578-9600 • Fax: 703-575-5400
Website: www.ascd.org • E-mail: member@ascd.org
Author guidelines: www.ascd.org/write

Judy Seltz, *Executive Director;* Stefani Roth, *Publisher;* Genny Ostertag, *Director, Content Acquisitions;* Julie Houtz, *Director, Book Editing & Production;* Darcie Russell, *Senior Associate Editor;* Lindsey Smith, *Senior Graphic Designer;* Mike Kalyan, *Manager, Production Services;* Valerie Younkin, *Production Designer;* Kyle Steichen, *Senior Production Specialist*

PAPERBACK ISBN: 978-1-4166-2049-5 ASCD product #115001

PDF E-BOOK ISBN: 978-1-4166-2051-8; see Books in Print for other formats.

Quantity discounts: 10–49, 10%; 50+, 15%; 1,000+, special discounts (e-mail programteam@ascd.org or call 800-933-2723, ext. 5773, or 703-575-5773). For desk copies, go to www.ascd.org/deskcopy.

ASCD Member Book No. FY15-8A (July 2015 PSI+). ASCD Member Books mail to Premium (P), Select (S), and Institutional Plus (I+) members on this schedule: Jan, PSI+; Feb, P; Apr, PSI+; May, P; Jul, PSI+; Aug, P; Sep, PSI+; Nov, PSI+; Dec, P. For current details on membership, see www.ascd.org/membership.

Library of Congress Cataloging-in-Publication Data

Vatterott, Cathy, 1951–
  Rethinking grading : meaningful assessment for standards-based learning / Cathy Vatterott.
    pages cm
  Includes bibliographical references and index.
  ISBN 978-1-4166-2049-5 (pbk. : alk. paper) 1. Grading and marking (Students)—United States. 2. Educational tests and measurements—United States. 3. Educational evaluation—United States. I. Title.
  LB3060.37.V37 2015
  371.27'2–dc23
                                2015009093

23 22 21 20 19 18 17 16 15   1 2 3 4 5 6 7 8 9 10 11 12

Rethinking Grading

MEANINGFUL ASSESSMENT FOR
STANDARDS-BASED LEARNING

• • •

Acknowledgments

My thanks go first to ASCD for an educational vision that has guided my career and for the forum it has provided for my ideas. I am honored to be an ASCD author. I also wish to thank Genny Ostertag, who served as my editor, coach, and taskmaster. She deftly navigated me through a series of twists, turns, delays, and rewrites to shape my ideas into a coherent manuscript. Her unrelenting encouragement and patience were invaluable. Thanks also to Darcie Russell, for smoothing the rough edges from my sometimes irreverent style and for her meticulous attention to detail.

I am beholden to all the authors who dared to question our most entrenched grading practices and whose research formed the foundation for the work of so many others. I have been particularly influenced by Alfie Kohn, Robert Lynn Canady, Tom Guskey, Ken O'Connor, Doug Reeves, and Tom Schimmer. Their writings, presentations, and personal conversations intrigued me, compelled me to reflect, and brought clarity to the big picture of grading.

Next, my thanks go out to those educators who befriended me during my research. I appreciate the thoughtfulness of my "grading buddies" Jeff Harding, Rob McEntarffer, Hugh O'Donnell, Matt Townsley, and Nathan Wear, who regularly took the time to chat with me and to share web links and articles they thought would help me. They remain great colleagues who have made the journey fun and exciting.

Finally, I am especially grateful to all the K–12 teachers and administrators who willingly gave me access to their expertise, their classrooms, and their grade books. I remain in awe of their energy, caring, and commitment to the students. They unselfishly gave of their time to teach me what standards-based grading looked like, and brought the concepts to life by sharing their practices. Their passion for standards-based grading was infectious and my visits with them never failed to energize me. They were my inspiration—without them, this book would not be possible.

• • •

Introduction

Grading. It's the hardest decision I must make in teaching. Every semester I agonize about what is right. Is the grade truly indicative of the student's performance? Do I have the weighting right? Have I given students enough opportunities to improve? All this happens within the confines of the amount of time and energy I have available to determine grades.

I continue to evolve in my practice. Last semester I created structured formative activities and rubrics. I found that those strategies helped more students "hit the mark" the first time. I had fewer rewrites with fewer deficiencies.

Writing this book has been an awakening. Each semester I am more thoughtful, more analytical, and more reflective about my own grading practices. At the same time, I am troubled by the mindset that my college freshmen and sophomores bring to my courses. (The juniors and seniors are a bit better.) For many, their K–12 experience has left them woefully unprepared to handle college-level work. They often don't fully comprehend how to analyze and synthesize. They seem to be stuck in the mode of "just tell me what you want." Many of them are terrible writers, unable to express their thoughts clearly and intelligently. I see firsthand the damage we have done, and how we have handicapped them for college by giving grades that don't reflect learning. I am not surprised by how many drop out.

We have the opportunity to change that. We have the opportunity to send students forward to college with the conceptual knowledge and learning strategies that are so critical to college success. It starts with empowering them to take charge of their own learning and by eliminating some of the obstacles of traditional grading. Standards-based grading has the potential to restore integrity to the grading process. It can and will change our students' futures.

1

The Culture of Grading

People are doing a lot of rethinking about education these days. The pundits agree that something is wrong with K–12 education, and everyone has a solution: a longer school day, a longer school year, more testing, less recess. Columnists, talk show hosts, and politicians on both sides lament that we've lost our edge. Competition is global and according to the tests we are not keeping up.

Why does global competitiveness matter? The intersection of globalization and technology has created an international competition for jobs and even college admissions. We can now easily compete, connect, and collaborate with people around the world (Friedman & Mandelbaum, 2012). "In today's interconnected world, our students are not competing with students from the state or city next door, but with students from Singapore, Shanghai, and Stockholm" (Stewart, 2012, p. 3). To be average is no longer good enough.

How are we doing? Some say there is a crisis in U.S. education. Others say the crisis is overblown. But there are some indisputable facts. On international tests, our students are performing poorly compared with students from other countries. Three international tests compare math, science, and reading performance—Trends in International Mathematics and Science Survey (TIMMS), Progress in International Reading Literacy Study (PIRLS), and the Programme for International Student Assessment (PISA). In 2011, U.S. 8th graders came in 7th place in math and 9th place in science on the TIMMS. In that same year, U.S. 4th graders ranked 6th out of 53 countries in reading on the PIRLS. PISA is the most widely used international test, measuring performance in 65 countries. It is also the most challenging in that its goal is to measure not merely content knowledge, but the ability of students to apply knowledge to solve real-life problems. On the PISA in 2012, U.S. students scored well below other developed countries—23rd in science, 30th in math, and 20th in reading (U. S. Department of Education, 2012a, 2012b, 2012c).

Even if we discount standardized test scores as an indicator of how our students are doing, we know this: In the United States, we not only have a *skills gap* (jobs that can't be filled due to a lack of skilled labor) but also a *learning gap* (an unacceptable high school and college dropout rate as well as college students who need remediation). The skills gap is evident in the lack of workers with specific skills needed for some of today's jobs, jobs that did not exist only a few years ago. In early 2012, in spite of the recession, there were more than three million jobs vacant in the United States due to a lack of math, reading comprehension, or technical skills required by companies (Friedman & Mandelbaum, 2012). The learning gap is twofold. First, 25 percent of our students will not graduate high school. The high school graduation rate in the United States of 74.7 percent ranks 12th among 28 developed countries (*Education Week*, 2013; Stewart, 2012). A high school diploma qualifies graduates for only a few low-wage jobs; adults without a high school diploma face dismal job prospects. Second, if U.S. students *do* make it to college, one-third of them must take at least one remedial course in reading, writing, or math. Only 54 percent of those entering college in the U.S. will complete a degree, ranking near the bottom when compared to other country's rates of college completion. Slots at elite universities are increasingly filled by better-prepared students from other countries.

People bemoan the sad state of U.S. competitiveness and insist that education is both the cause and the fix of our woes. Yet no one seems to have a definitive answer about what in education needs to be fixed. No one has the answer because there isn't just one answer. It's a series of related problems that overlap among curriculum, instruction, and assessment.

Although K–12 educational reform is not the cure-all for the ills of the United States, the reform of one educational practice—grading—has the potential to drive related changes in other practices. The culture of grading and all the baggage it encompasses has perpetuated a system that obstructs many other educational reforms. What is the relationship between grading reform and overall educational reform? Are grades a *reflection* of a dysfunctional system or a *driver* of the system? Hard to say. Grades are supposed to reflect what students know and how well the teacher has taught. But they often don't.

We now know that something is wrong with grades. Every day we see the mismatch—on one hand, the stellar performance on standardized tests from *B* and *C* students (thus labeled "under-achievers"), and on the other, poor performance on standardized tests from straight *A* students. We know that many students leave high school with high grade point averages yet struggle academically in college.

Let us reflect for a moment on the "what ifs"—that perhaps the answer lies in the reform of a traditional educational practice that has not changed in decades. What if grading practices were a piece of a bigger picture? What if by changing the way we use grades we could ignite authentic high-level learning? What if student empowerment could make learning more dynamic and change the outcome? What if our beliefs about grading were misguided?

If we dare to question our beliefs about grading, more "what if" questions emerge.

- What if an *A* student was a compliant one rather than a learned one?
- What if the premise that high grades were a predictor of success in life was faulty?
- What if grades, as the marker of success in school, were a flawed, or worse yet, meaningless tool?
- What if parents, by directing their children to focus on grades, inadvertently created an addiction to form over substance?

The challenge of reforming grading practices is a difficult one. The "what ifs" reveal a practice that is deeply ingrained not only in education but in our culture. Grading is a language, a schema— we grade presidents and we grade meat. For grading reform to happen, we must acknowledge and accept how our beliefs have influenced grading practices.

A Brief History of Education

How did we get here? Three historical forces converged to create and perpetuate traditional grading practices that are common today—the roots of education in moral development, the use of education to sort and rank students, and the prevalence of behaviorism in school practices.

Teacher as Moral Educator

In a young and often chaotic colonial America, moral stability was necessary for the survival of society. The original establishment of schools was primarily for the purpose of moral education, and schools were viewed as an important social agency to promote virtue, character, and good habits. From the earliest days of our country, the goal of mass literacy was driven by the need to

read the Bible and thus save one's soul. Contrary to today's practice of secular education, schools were the servant of religion, and
moral education in the schools was a logical outgrowth of religion.
"In the eyes of Puritans religious and moral education were inex-
tricably intertwined" (McClellan, 1999, p. 2). Learning was valued
not as an end in itself but as "an instrument for clarifying the ways
of God to man and thus rendering certain the conditions of eternal
salvation" (Thayer, 1965, p. 12). Teachers worked hard to promote
in students the virtues of self-restraint, industry, honesty, punctuality, and orderliness. Discipline in school was viewed as a way to
model full obedience to God.

A basic fear of the fragility of human virtue pervaded our society—that without constraints and vigilance our youth would fall
prey to unsavory temptations. This fear was grounded in the 17th
century conception of original sin, that man was predisposed to
choose evil over good (Thayer, 1965). The fears of our founding
fathers were not much different from the general concerns for
our youth today, and the roots of moral education are evident in
today's common educational practices. We reward the modern
version of virtue and punish the lack of it. We reward responsibility, effort, hard work, neatness, and homework completion. We
penalize tardiness, sloppiness, late work, and cheating. For this
noble goal of instilling morality in students, grades have been a
most convenient tool. Unfortunately, this use of grades has led to
a school culture that often places more value on compliance and
working than learning.

Schools as a Mechanism for Sorting and Ranking

Early in the 20th century, compulsory attendance laws
changed the practice of K–12 education in the United States.
Elementary schools grew in popularity and large numbers of students started attending high school. From 1870 to 1910 the number of high schools in the United States grew from 500 to 10,000,
and the total number of students in public elementary and high

schools grew from 6,871,000 to 17,813,000 (Kirschenbaum, Simon, & Napier, 1971). While elementary schools continued to report student learning with narratives, the sheer number of students at the secondary level made such descriptive reports burdensome. Secondary schools, eager for a more efficient alternative, began examining techniques used in colleges.

In the late 1700s, Yale was probably the first college to rank student performance into four categories, a practice that evolved into the use of a four-point scale (a precursor of the four-point grade point average). In 1877, Harvard began classifying students using percentages, which was later replaced by classifying students into five groups, the lowest of which failed the class (Durm, 1993). In 1897, Mount Holyoke College adopted a system that combined descriptive adjectives with percentages and letters:

> *A* = Excellent, equivalent to 95–100 percent
> *B* = Good, equivalent to 85–94 percent
> *C* = Fair, equivalent to 76–84 percent
> *D* = Passed (barely), equivalent to 75 percent
> *E* = Failed (below 75 percent) (Durm, 1993, p. 3)

This system of grading, with variations from school to school, evolved to become the standard for sorting and ranking college students and was soon adopted by secondary schools. Letter grades were an easy, efficient method not only for telling students how they were doing, but also for ability-grouping students for instruction. As the number of high school students applying to college increased, colleges starting using high school grades to screen applicants.

In 1912, some powerful research emerged about the lack of consistency in percentage grades. When English exams from two students were scored by 142 different teachers, the scores on one exam ranged from 64 to 98 percent and scores on the other exam ranged from 50 to 97 percent. The same experiment with geometry papers showed even more discrepancy, with the grades ranging from 28 to 95 percent (Starch & Elliott, 1912, 1913). This research was viewed as so damaging to the practice of using percentages that educators began moving away from the 100-point scale to the five categories of *A, B, C, D*, and *F*. Fewer categories seemed more "fair."

Around this time, a new method became popular—grading on the curve. The bell curve, technically called the *normal distribution*, can actually be traced back to the work of statisticians and mathematicians as early as the 18th century. It became popular in the 20th century after it was shown that many physical and psychological phenomena (such as height) presented as a normal distribution. The use of the bell curve in education became popular when IQ scores of a random group of children were shown to fall into a bell-shaped curve (Curreton, 1971; Jensen, 1980). Grading on the curve was believed to be appropriate because, at that time, the distribution of students' intelligence test scores approximated a normal probability curve. Since innate intelligence and school achievement were thought to be directly related, such a procedure seemed both fair and equitable (Guskey, 1996). The assumption that individual aptitude was fixed and that aptitude varied among students led to the logical conclusion that achievement should also present as a bell curve. Regardless of its validity, the bell curve became popular as a way to produce a "fair" distribution of grades. For the purpose of sorting and ranking students, the bell curve was ideal.

Upon closer investigation, however, the logic was shown to be faulty. The normal curve was not considered statistically valid unless the group was large, random, and untreated (Kelly, 2009). "The normal bell-shaped curve describes the distribution of randomly occurring events *when nothing intervenes*" (Guskey, 2011, p. 18). But teachers intervene—they teach with the goal of having all students learn. "If the distribution of student learning after teaching resembles a normal bell-shaped curve, that, too, shows the degree to which our intervention failed. It made no difference" (Guskey, 2011, p. 18). More recent research has also shown that the relationship between aptitude/intelligence and school achievement is dependent upon the appropriateness of instructional conditions (Hanushek, 2004; Hershberg, 2005). "When the instructional quality is high and well matched to students' learning needs, the magnitude of the relationship between aptitude/intelligence and school achievement diminishes drastically and approaches zero" (Guskey, 2011, p. 18). In spite of this fact, the bell curve is still mistakenly revered today as evidence of rigor.

Behaviorism as a Tool for Compliance

If morality and sorting and ranking were what we wanted, behaviorism was the way to reach the goal.

> You may find the roots of behaviorism and its counterpart in education, behavior modification, to have germinated from some unusual sources—a salivating dog, a ringing bell, and, more recently, some chocolate covered candies. (Freiberg, 1999, p. 5)

Behaviorism, a major contribution to the field of psychology, dates back to the late 17th century. At that time, Edward Thorndike theorized about the Law of Effect, that behavior leading to a positive consequence will be repeated (Kohn, 1999). Skinner's theory of operant conditioning showed that human behavior could be shaped through positive reinforcement. For example, the practice of placing chocolate candies on students' desks was used to reinforce good behavior (Freiberg, 1999).

Pavlov learned that he could get a dog to salivate simply by associating the sound of a ringing bell with food. Pavlov won the Nobel Prize in 1904 for his study of digestion, but the research was applied to a new psychological theory for humans (Freiberg, 1999). As behaviorism grew in popularity, it led to a new approach to classroom management. Behavior modification emerged in the

1960s and rapidly became the dominant philosophy for classroom management. One of the more popular programs was Lee Canter's Assertive Discipline.

Canter's Assertive Discipline model was a structure of rewards and consequences that were used to control student behavior. The most familiar consequence for bad behavior was that of writing the student's name on the board, followed by check marks behind the name for each additional infraction. The name on the board was meant as a warning, the check mark as a consequence. "If you do break this rule again, or any other rule during the day, I'll put a check next to your name... this means that you have chosen to sit for five minutes in the time-out area" (Canter & Canter, 1992, p. 103). A popular reward for good behavior was Marbles in a Jar.

> When the class is doing what you want, you take a marble and drop it in a jar. The sound of the marble dropping into the jar immediately lets the students know they are doing what you want and that you recognize their efforts. Each marble can be worth, for example, 30 seconds to one minute of free choice at the end of the day. (Canter, 1976, p. 141)

The widespread use of behavior modification for classroom management generalized to other school practices such as detentions for misbehavior, awards for perfect attendance, and even the use of bells (particularly ironic in light of Pavlov). Behavior management became the dominant paradigm in schools for controlling the *behavior* of learning (or so we thought) as well as controlling classroom behavior.

Today the idea that behavior can be controlled by rewards and punishment is so embedded in the day-to-day practices of schools, one rarely even notices it (Kohn, 1999). Given the fact that "behaviorism permeates virtually every aspect of American education" (Kohn, 1999, p. 143), it is no surprise that grades have become a major tool for rewarding good. So although grades originally evolved for the purpose of sorting and ranking, they turned out to be quite handy for rewarding virtue and punishing vice. They were an all-purpose tool—for rewarding not only achievement but behaviors such as compliance and responsibility.

Beliefs About Grading

From the historical forces of morality, sorting, and behaviorism, a culture of grading evolved that was a mix of moralistic views of human nature, the puritan work ethic, and the use of reward and punishment to shape behavior. The culture is evident in a set of beliefs about grading, the quasi-superstitions that drive educational practice. Those beliefs developed from the most honorable motives. As educators we have been concerned not only about intellectual growth, but also moral development and the preparation of children for adulthood. We've used grades for more than academics because we believe our job is more than academics—our goals have always included shaping children into better people. But our well-meaning beliefs and their unintended consequences deserve closer examination.

Belief #1: Good Teachers Give Bad Grades

As we accepted that the role of the school was to sort and rank, we came to believe that in a rigorous educational system, success was scarce. Scarcity of high grades equaled rigor and only a few should be "winners." (A student once said to her professor, "Well, if everyone got an *A*, then it doesn't mean anything.") From a practical standpoint, we also realized if there were too many high grades, sorting and ranking students would be difficult.

The bell curve became the foundation for academic competition—it became synonymous with academic rigor. We accepted the bell curve as an indication of some natural order of things. We were confident our belief in it was valid, because, after all, the bell curve was science. If the purpose of grading was to rank and discriminate poor learners from good learners, then the closer the grades approximated a bell-shaped curve, the better. If we set the standard for excellence so high that only a few students excelled and many failed, then we must have very high standards. Then, of course, the inverse must be true—lots of high grades must indicate low standards and a watered-down curriculum. (As a first-year teacher, I was called to the principal's office to be chastised for giving too many *A*s, until I explained that I taught for mastery, with formative feedback and retakes).

As teachers, we bought into the idea that a bell curve indicated rigor and misinterpreted it to be a *rule to follow* (any idea can be bastardized!). We came to believe that if success were scarce and grades fell into a bell curve, then we were tough teachers. The grades became our yardstick—a measure of how tough we were and a measure of how tough the content was. This belief became so commonplace that nearly all college students have had the experience on the first day of class when the professor proudly announces "half of you will fail this class." When enough students did not fail, the teacher or the curriculum was labeled "too easy" (Vatterott, 2007). We even have a name for it—grade inflation.

In 1894, only a decade after Harvard adopted letter grades, a group of professors began complaining that "grades *A* and *B* are sometimes given too readily" (Goodwin, 2011, p. 80). The concept of grade inflation has been with us ever since. Grade inflation is derived from the belief that rigor equals a scarcity of high grades and that the purpose of grading is to sort and rank. Grade inflation is assumed to be present when grades or grade point averages go up without a similar rise in achievement (Kohn, 2002; Zirkel, 2007). The belief is that if there are too many high grades, then they must be less accurate or not deserved. But higher grades could indeed be accurate.

> It is not a symbol of rigor to have grades fall into a "normal" distribution, rather it is a symbol of failure—failure to teach well, failure to test well, and failure to have any influence at all on

the intellectual lives of students. (Milton, Pollio, & Eison, 1986, p. 209)

This decades-old debate won't be resolved as long as it is framed in terms of the "normal" or "bell" curve. Making this the first premise for grading students reflects a serious misunderstanding of this statistical concept. (Kelly, 2009, p. 696)

In the days before differentiation, when all students were taught one way and given the same amount of time to learn, this variation in achievement was easily accomplished. Teachers began to take pride in the ability of a test to discriminate and yield a bell-shaped distribution of grades. If necessary, conditions could easily be contrived to create a bell curve. There was no trick to giving bad grades—any teacher could make a test so hard that only a few students got *A*s. In an effort to make learning more rigorous, teachers often just created *more* work. But often that work was not more intellectually challenging. The *more is always better* argument ignored the quality of work and level of learning required (Vatterott, 2007). Rigor and difficulty was often equated to the amount of work done by students rather than the complexity and challenge of the work (Williamson & Johnston, 1999).

Institutionalizing failure. Unfortunately, sorting and ranking learners became a pervasive practice and a most formidable obstacle to student success (Canady & Hotchkiss, 1989). In far too many schools, the bell-shaped curve became the icon of sorting and ranking—it dictated programs and created the tradition of norm comparisons. The bell curve set up "unnecessary and counterproductive scarcities of student success in competitive, win-lose environments" (Bonstingl, 1992, p. 7).

Use of the bell curve led to an acceptance of student failure—educators began to make plans for some students to fail. Schools established policies for retaining elementary students and developed programs for alternative schools and credit recovery for secondary students. Such practices reinforced the belief that some students could not learn and perpetuated a system that not only allowed for but actually expected failure. In the sorting and ranking system, when failure did occur, it was viewed as the fault of the student and the blame was placed squarely there. The belief was that there was something wrong with those students and they needed to be fixed. In many ways, sorting and ranking practices institutionalized failure and conveniently absolved teachers of the responsibility for student failure (Vatterott, 2007).

Belief #2: Not Everyone Deserves an *A*

Born from our roots as moral educators and our fondness for sorting and ranking, the concept of an *A* student is embedded in our culture as an icon of discipline, responsibility, and hard work. Many people feel strongly that grades should reflect more than learning. We view grades as a package deal; to succeed, students must have it all—academic achievement *and* moral virtues. An *A* student is one who is not only smart—he or she must be learned *and* virtuous. For many teachers, that's what an *A* student is.

This belief is played out in schools every year. Here are a few common scenarios:

Jimmy, a surly and difficult 7th grader, is regularly sent to the office for disrespect and fighting. He is often absent, yet manages to make good grades on in-class work and tests. After absences, he fails to contact the teacher to make up missing work. Due to zeros for missing work, he is receiving *D*s in several classes. It is May and time for retention decisions. In spite of evidence that he has mastered the 7th grade curriculum, his academic team of teachers wants to retain him in the 7th grade "because he doesn't *deserve* to be promoted to the 8th grade."

Zack, a popular high school senior, is considered an excellent student. He consistently earns *A*s and *B*s and recently received a scholarship to Cornell. It's the end of the school year and he has a take-home exam due for his literature class. The exam counts

40 percent of his final course grade. Even though the exam demonstrates his mastery of the content at an *A* level, because the assignment was turned in a day late, he receives a zero. Zack may fail the class and his scholarship at Cornell may be in jeopardy. Last year in a similar situation with the same teacher, a student's acceptance to college was rescinded based on the effect of this practice on his final grade point average.

Some teachers feel it is their duty to sort and rank by intellect and virtue, that they have an obligation to society to "separate the wheat from the chaff." But as the scenarios show, sometimes their efforts result in decisions that adversely affect students.

Belief #3: Grades Motivate Learners

The belief that grades motivate learners was a logical extension of educators' homage to behaviorism. This belief has evolved from a series of misconceptions. The first misconception is that learning is only a means to an end—to escape punishment or get a reward, that learning has no intrinsic value, and that students would not be interested in learning for its own sake. If learning is an inherently distasteful process, then students must be coerced and grades can be a method of coercion (Stiggins, 2005; Vatterott, 2007). How sad if this were truly the case.

The second misconception is that a single entity called motivation exists, that students either have it or don't have it, and it can be manipulated by external forces (behaviorism again!) (Glasser, 1992; Stiggins, 2005). In other words, it is possible to motivate someone to do something they don't want to do, given the right sort of carrots and sticks. The third misconception is that the most effective method is the use of rewards and/or punishment (as opposed to engagement, relevance, or meaningful tasks) and that grades are an effective reward and/or punishment for all students. Most teachers have come to realize that good grades motivate students who value good grades and bad grades don't motivate anyone, with the possible exception of a few over-achievers (Vatterott, 2007).

Unlike Pavlov's dogs, children are not primitive creatures who respond only to reward and punishment. They are complex thinking, feeling beings with a natural curiosity that we must be careful not to extinguish. And learning is not merely a behavior—it is a complex mental process that is mediated by many factors and is unique in each child.

Grades as Commodity

Our beliefs have led to an abuse of grades. What began as a way to sort and reflect the quality of learning has evolved into an obsession, the weapon of choice for teachers, and a prized commodity for students and parents. In the behaviorist tradition, children are bribed, punished, and rewarded for the letters on the report card. Children and parents worship grades as the measure of a student's success. To them, grades have come to represent the relative value of a learner (regardless of the criteria used to arrive at the grade).

To students, grades have come to represent how hard they worked and how well they followed the rules. Students are quick to protest a grade that might actually reflect learning, if it is incongruent with their idea of what a grade means. For one student, the complaint went like this: "I attended every class and demonstrated an exemplary amount of participation. I was under the impression that I would earn an *A* with the effort I had applied." *Under the impression* is exactly our problem. Students have come to believe that effort (however weak), not learning, earns them the *A*. To parents, good grades reassure them that their child is a smart and successful student. We intensify the value of the grade by awarding honor roll status to the top grade-getters and affix stickers to our cars that state "My child is an honor roll student at Meadowbrook Elementary School." In response, other cars sport bumper stickers that say "My kid can beat up your honor student" or "My dog is smarter than your honor student."

Truth be told, we like our norm-based comparisons. As a competitive culture, we *like* winners and losers and the fact that there is only so much room at the top. It is a way to demonstrate (we believe) that school is a meritocracy—that hard work is rewarded, and that a hierarchy of achievement exists. This system secures the fate of those few at the top, who are then given access to the best high schools and colleges. So the tradition of honor rolls, class rank, and valedictorians lives on.

Grades do reflect a meritocracy, but it's the wrong meritocracy. What is the merit? Is it learning, completion of all assigned tasks, compliance, or responsibility? A true meritocracy based only on learning would require an attitudinal shift. It would require us to let go of those other qualities we value in students, or at least agree to count them differently.

In our relentless pursuit of the almighty *A* and the perfect GPA, something got lost—learning. Grades became the be-all and end-all, the goal itself, not an indicator of achieving the goal of learning. Grades have become the commodity, the badge of success and smarts, the ticket to college. But what do they really mean?

Forces Driving Change

Grades are often not an authentic reflection of learning. The way we currently use grades contributes to other problems in education. If changing grading practices could precipitate broader changes in teaching and learning, it's possible that our mediocre academic standing in the world could be greatly improved. Now is the time for change. Cultural and educational forces have created the perfect storm for changing grading practices. These forces compel us to action. These forces provide us with a much-needed reality check about grades.

Reality Check #1: No Child Left Behind

Our earliest reality check came when No Child Left Behind (NCLB) became part of our world. With NCLB came accountability. Oh, wait—we need to worry about what our students *learn*, not just how well they *obey*? We can no longer simply fail those who don't learn and move on? "All must be proficient," NCLB said. This was a foreign concept to teachers—we had never been expected to ensure that all students were proficient. We didn't know *how* to do that. We were not even sure that it was possible. There were *always* some that failed. Wasn't that what rigor meant? We were accustomed to institutionalized failure. Then when we attempted to implement the concept of "no child left behind," we did it within the old sort-and-rank system. We taught them one way and didn't know how to differentiate, or if it was even fair to differentiate. We were stuck in a mindset of the past—that told us to sort and rank and to create a bell-shaped curve; a mindset that told us that success was supposed to be rare, not common; a mindset that told us that some were destined to fail.

The movement for learning proficiency revealed that what we thought grades meant was an illusion. If we accepted that standardized tests, flawed as they were, did reflect *some* measure of student learning, then the mismatch between the grades students were receiving and *actual* learning was stark. NCLB exposed a dirty little secret—*grades don't equate with performance on standardized tests*. Some students who were compliant and hard workers got good grades but did poorly on the standardized tests. Some students tested well but received poor grades because of missing assignments, late work, or bad behavior.

We came to realize that often grades didn't reflect proficiency in learning at all. With so many factors other than learning clouding the grade, it was hard to say what the grade meant. For students it became a chess game—a game of moves and strategies to get the grade. The further students progressed in school, the better they became at the game; the better they became at "doing school" (Pope, 2001). By high school, students were quite adept at manipulating the system, cheating, and taking short cuts, all to get the grade.

> An *A* grade, therefore, did not necessarily mean that the students learned and retained content area knowledge and skills or that they understood important concepts or theories: rather, the grades proved that the students were adept at providing the teachers with the information required on tests and quizzes, and that they had memorized these facts and figures (or copied them from peers) just long enough to "ace" the exams and then move on to the next set of tasks. (Pope, 2001, p. 156)

Accountability for learning demands grades that are reflective of learning.

Reality Check #2: Grades Are Misleading About Succeeding

The implicit promise of good grades goes like this—if you work hard and get good grades, then you'll be successful in life. Good grades are viewed as a marker of success and responsibility, and our culture routinely rewards them as such. Parents pay cold hard cash, schools give away baseball tickets, and local businesses routinely give discounts for good grades. A puzzling example is that good grades in high school earn students cheaper car insurance. Why—because good students are safer drivers or because good grades mean you are an accomplished rule-follower who will follow the rules of the road?

Parents and students obsess about grades as the ticket to a better future. But do good grades correlate with future academic success? Yes and no. First, the good news. Yes, good grades in high school do correlate with ACT scores and first-year college grades. There is a clear and consistent relationship between high school grade point average and scores on the ACT—as the score on the ACT rises, so does the average high school grade point average for that score (ACT, 2005). There is, however, evidence that high school GPAs have been rising at a proportionately higher rate than scores on the ACT (Zirkel, 2007). One indicator is that the average high school GPA associated with specific scores on the ACT has risen. From 1991 to 2003, the average high school GPA of students receiving a composite score of 20 on the ACT rose from 2.85 to 3.10. For students earning a composite score of 28, the average high school GPA rose from 3.5 to 3.65 (ACT, 2005).

> Between 1991 and 2003, the mathematics grades of high school students taking the ACT exam rose from a grade point average of 2.80 to 3.04, whereas their average score on the math portion of the ACT rose only slightly, from 20.04 to 20.55 on a 36 point scale. (Goodwin, 2011, p. 80)

A similar relationship was shown in ACT English scores when compared to high school English grade point averages. In another comparison, although student high school grades in reading rose between 1992 and 2005, student scores on the reading portion of the National Assessment of Educational Progress (NAEP) declined (Schmidt, 2007).

What about the correlation between high school grades and college grades? Both high school grade point average and ACT scores correlate with college grades and successful completion of the freshman year (Beecher & Fischer, 1999; Geiser & Santelices, 2007). "ACT and high school grade point average seem to be effective predictors of college success regardless of course content because they are indicators of generic abilities and motivation" (Beecher & Fischer, 1999, p. 4). In other words, the relationship may exist because students have learned how to get good grades, not necessarily because they took more challenging courses in high school.

Now for the bad news. Grades are misleading when it comes to predicting success because high grades may help students *get into* college, but they don't necessarily prepare them academically to *succeed* in college. The reality is that in the United States,

30 percent of freshmen at four-year institutions will drop out (Goodwin, 2011) and only 54 percent of students entering college will complete a degree (Stewart, 2012). Interestingly, when college graduation rates are correlated with high school grade point averages, students with GPAs below 3.25 have graduation rates at 44 percent or lower. Only students with GPAs above 3.25 show graduation rates of above 50 percent (OIRP, 2011). The higher the high school GPA, the better predictor it is for college graduation (Stumpf & Stanley, 2002). But a college graduation rate of 54 percent is still a dismal figure.

High school students, busy chasing the grade, often arrive at college without a solid academic foundation to succeed in college classes. "Too many students now enter with advanced courses on their résumés but little grasp of the all-important basics" (Oxtoby, 2007, p. 43).

When looking at a high school transcript, it is impossible to know whether a *B* in high school chemistry indicates the student understood 80 percent of the concepts or that the student understood little and padded poor test grades with copied homework and extra credit.

> About a third of first-year students entering college had taken at least one remedial course for reading, writing, or math. The number is even higher for black and Hispanic students. At public two-year colleges, that average number rises to above 40 percent. And having to take just one remedial course is highly correlated with failure to graduate from college. (Friedman & Mandelbaum, 2012, p. 116)

By focusing on the high grade point average for college admission, some students have been shortchanged in learning, inadvertently making them *less* prepared academically while making them very talented at working the system. We thought that we were rewarding the right thing—completion of tasks, compliance, promptness. But in that process if we devalued mastery of deep conceptual learning, we have hampered students' future success. Maybe the grading practices that we *thought* were preparing students for the future really weren't.

Reality Check #3:
The Common Core State Standards Change Everything

The initiative for the Common Core State Standards originated with the nation's governors and education commissioners, through their representative organizations, the National Governors Association (NGA) and the Council of Chief State School Officers (CCSSO). At this writing, 45 states have agreed to implement these standards (www.corestandards.org). The goal of the standards is to prepare students for the future, to ensure that all students are college and career ready, and that they are able to compete in the global economy. The standards attempt to raise the bar for what students know and are able to do. The standards go beyond previous standards in that they require students to use and apply complex knowledge and skills to solve unfamiliar problems. This level of application of knowledge and skills is one area in which U.S. students are particularly lacking. For instance, on international tests, U.S. students fared relatively better on the TIMMS in part because the multiple-choice questions asked them to reproduce curriculum content. They did relatively poorly on PISA, which required them to apply knowledge to real-life situations (Stewart, 2012). Those results exposed another dirty little secret in U.S. education. Although standards and standardized tests have supposedly driven instruction for years, we now see that *we have been focusing too much on low-level rote learning.*

Too often, we have neither allowed nor expected students to think. We have filled their heads with facts and formulas and rewarded them for reciting it. *We* have done the analyzing, synthesizing, and evaluating instead of expecting our students to do it. *We* have done too much of the work of learning, perhaps because we didn't trust them to *want* to do the work, or perhaps because we weren't sure they were *able* to do the work. This failure to require higher-level thinking is part of the reason our students are not prepared for college. (After assigning a synthesis-level task to my college sophomores, I was dismayed to have a student ask, "Where do I find the answer?" "You have to create it!" I replied.)

Putting it bluntly, our definitions of what it means to teach and what it means to learn are outdated and simplistic. Our expectations have been seriously out of sync with what the future will demand of our students. The implementation of the standards should change that. They will affect not only what we teach, but how we teach, and how we assess what students have learned. (The effects of standards will be discussed more fully in Chapters 3 and 4.) To successfully navigate the standards, student grades will need to reflect mastery of skills, not memory of content. This goal is congruent with the skills students will need to succeed in a new world.

Preparing Students for the New World

The world we are preparing our students for has changed. In the past we were preparing them for an industrial world and top-down management—obey, meet deadlines, follow rigid rules, punch the time clock. Today we must prepare them for a world in which they must know how to take initiative, self-advocate, solve problems, be creative, and accomplish tasks without minute-to-minute supervision. Tomorrow's jobs will require critical thinking, sophisticated communication skills, handling nonroutine complex tasks, and working collaboratively with others to solve problems (Friedman & Mandelbaum, 2011; Stewart, 2012). As the world has changed, the outcomes we want for education must change. We need students to be both college and career ready. What skills and dispositions are needed? The standards have defined them. Students who are college and career ready

- are motivated to learn independently of external rewards and punishments.
- are self-directed learners who know how to assess their own learning needs.
- are inclined to seek out and use resources to assist them in learning.
- exhibit a willingness to try, persistence, and a belief that effort will pay off in eventual success (www.corestandards. org).

Many traditional educational practices, such as rote learning and the use of grades as reward and punishment, have interfered with, if not prevented, the development of these essential skills and dispositions in students. We must reexamine our teaching, learning, and assessment practices to decide which type of student we want to produce.

- Do we want students who can memorize and repeat or students who can analyze, synthesize, and problem solve?
- Do we want students who are excited and engaged and involved in their learning or students who obediently slog through whatever tasks they are given?
- Do we want students whose goal is to get the grade at any cost or to find meaning in what they do?

The kind of students we produce will determine the kind of adults who will inhabit the United States and our global community. Chapter 2 will examine in detail how traditional grading practices hinder the development of the skills our students need for a successful future.

2

Why We Need
a New Grading Paradigm

Standards-based grading is not just about changing grading—it's a complete overhaul of the teaching-learning process. Curriculum, instruction, learning, and assessment differ from the traditional system. The paradigm shift is a shift from a compliance culture driven by teacher power—where grades rewarded compliance and punished noncompliance—to a performance culture driven by student empowerment and mastery of learning. The standards-based grading paradigm is different from the traditional grading paradigm in four major ways:

1. how learning is defined
2. how learning is structured
3. how learning is experienced
4. how grades are used

How Learning Is Defined

In the old paradigm, learning could easily be described as "stuff." A throwback to earlier times when books were rare and all knowledge needed to be retained in one's mind, students routinely had to memorize state capitals, names and dates of battles, and even poetry to perform well on tests of rote knowledge. Equating remembering with learning and with being smart is a long-standing tradition. When the scarecrow finally got a brain in *The Wizard of Oz,* he rattled off mathematical formulas. Television game shows routinely reward low-level rote knowledge and influence our concept of what it means to be "smarter than a 5th grader." Given the pervasiveness of this view, it is not surprising that many teachers still fixate on the coverage of rote knowledge and still equate remembering with learning. Often requiring students only to know and understand, many teachers have not expected students to function at the levels of application, analysis, and synthesis. Many teachers are not sure *how to teach* for higher-level thinking and many students don't know *how to think* at higher levels because they have not been expected to do so.

The new standards-based paradigm is really a new philosophy that redefines learning. Learning is defined by the standards—not by what students *know*, but by what they can *do with what they know.* Teachers can no longer just give all the information to students and expect it to be regurgitated. Evidence of learning is not repeating information but demonstrating the action of the standard. The Common Core State Standards (CCSS) reflect this philosophy: they are not content based, but skill based. Learning has moved from micro to macro, from a focus on content to a focus on skills, and from lower-order thinking skills to higher-order thinking skills (Herman & Linn, 2014). This new paradigm of learning demands that students *think* their way to understanding, be able to use tools in new situations, and be able to apply skills to solving real-world problems. In the old paradigm, students had been putting widgets into holes on an assembly line—now we are asking them to build the car.

In the old paradigm, rigor was evidenced by the amount of content a teacher covered and the ability of students to commit large bodies of factual knowledge to memory. In the new standards-based paradigm, rigor is defined not by the quantity of knowledge covered, but by the complexity of tasks and the level of mastery of higher-level thinking skills that students can attain. This new definition of learning has implications for how instruction is structured and organized. The differences in the paradigms are shown in Figure 2.1.

Figure 2.1   How Learning Is Defined

Traditional Grading Paradigm	Standards-Based Grading Paradigm
Low-level rote knowledge	Higher-order thinking skills
Knowing and understanding	Applying, analyzing, synthesizing
Learning defined by what students know	Learning defined by what students can do with what they know
Evidence of learning is repeating back	Evidence of learning is using skills in new situations
Rigor is coverage	Rigor is complexity

How Learning Is Structured

In the old paradigm, all students were treated the same, with all students in a grade level completing the same curriculum within the same amount of time. Learning was organized in such a way that all students received the same instruction (typically in a class group), the same homework, and the same test. Teachers assumed their methods of instruction and learning tasks were infallible—that they would work for all students. The assumption was that all students could learn in the same amount of time and in the same way. We believed the amount of time we gave students to learn was adequate, and therefore it was appropriate to test all students one time, at the same moment in time, and record grades as permanent. This practice amounted to one-shot learning: you need to know it Tuesday at 10:00 a.m. In the old paradigm, we taught, we tested, and we moved on.

As we now understand, however, when all students are treated the same and when the time for learning is fixed, *achievement varies*. In the old paradigm, students who learned easily from the standard method of instruction succeeded, and students who required a different method or more time achieved less and were penalized for it. Speed of learning came to be equated with intelligence. Treating all students the same resulted in a certain percentage of students who failed (DeLorenzo, Battino, Schreiber, & Gaddy Carrio, 2009; Vatterott, 2007).

The Rhythm of Learning in the Standards-Based Paradigm

The rhythm of learning in the old paradigm is reminiscent of a team of rowers, all in the same boat, rowing in unison. But in the standards-based paradigm, we understand that different students require different paths and varying amounts of time to learn, ideally to reach the same end. Standards-based learning is not linear—groups of students branch off in different directions based on their learning needs (Tomlinson, 2014). Learning is differentiated to enable all students to reach the same level of proficiency of the standards. Instead of teach, test, and move on in one large group, learning is a series of masteries for individual students—teach, check for understanding, apply learning, get feedback, revise learning, and get more feedback until mastery is achieved. Learning looks more like a spiral (the squiggly icing on a cupcake comes to mind), with students looping back for additional help. Unlike the old paradigm of one-shot learning, a feedback loop exists that makes learning dynamic—feedback to the students informs their learning and teachers change instruction as they see what individual students need.

In the standards-based paradigm, time to learn varies but achievement is fixed. We move away from a set amount of time with many students reaching relatively low levels of academic performance to one in which students move in a self-paced manner to reach high levels of academic performance (DeLorenzo et al., 2009). Teachers respect that the time it takes to learn varies from one student to the next; we move from all students marching in a lockstep group to individual students progressing at different rates (Tomlinson, 2008). The process may look different for different students. Some students learn quickly, proceeding through the curriculum in a straight line. Other students' learning looks more like stair steps, with periods where learning is stalled and where they need additional practice or reteaching. Still others work for long periods before the light bulb goes on.

In the standards-based classroom, daily instruction looks different from traditional whole-class instruction. Students receive corrective feedback from the teacher, other students, or computers. Methods of learning are differentiated, and there may be multiple small groups of students working on different tasks at the same time. Learning is constantly being assessed and reassessed—assessment is a continuous process, not a moment-in-time event. As a result, learning is more efficient and more students achieve mastery. The differences in the paradigms are shown in Figure 2.2.

How Learning Is Experienced

Perhaps the worst damage done in the traditional grading paradigm is the damage to student motivation and how students personally experience grades. When all grades are permanent, students have one chance to get it right. That system creates a perception that learning is supposed to be error-free. If that is the case, then students don't feel comfortable admitting they don't understand something and they are afraid to ask for help. It doesn't feel right to express frustration or confusion. Although they are still learning something, they are punished with a low grade if they don't get it right away—mistakes made while learning are penalized. Within the traditional grading paradigm, it's not safe to make mistakes.

Figure 2.2   How Learning Is Structured

Traditional Grading Paradigm	Results	Standards-Based Grading Paradigm	Results
• Whole class—all get the same instruction, same homework, same test	• Only students who learn well from that method succeed	• Learning is differentiated to enable mastery	• Learning is more efficient
• Time to learn fixed/achievement varies	• Learners who need more time are penalized	• Time to learn varies/achievement fixed	• More students achieve mastery
• One-shot learning (do you know it Tuesday at 10:00 a.m.?) • Grades are permanent • Teach → test → move on	• Speed = intelligence	• Assessment is a continuous process • Feedback loop: → Teach → check → apply learning → feedback	• "I can keep working and take the assessment when I am confident that I understand"

The hidden message that is internalized by the student is a *fixed mindset*—"I'm just not smart" (Dweck, 2007). In the traditional paradigm, failure is a judgment and a validation of a student's lack of ability. When it's not OK to make mistakes, students spend a great deal of energy avoiding imperfection and trying to look smart. This encourages deception, inhibits risk taking, and breeds a fear of failure and a false sense of shame ("I must be stupid"). The patterns of school failure in the traditional system tend to reinforce the fixed mindset as the same students fail over and over again. As those students come to believe they're just not smart, the mindset becomes a self-fulfilling prophecy. Struggling students begin to avoid learning. "Given all this, why persist?" they say. For the struggling learner, failure feels like *fait accompli*—a permanent caste system for *C* students and below.

These student attitudes can sabotage the critical quality of perseverance that we hope to develop in students. To make matters worse, when students don't learn right away, teachers often lower their expectations. With the kindest of motives, they offer lightning-fast rescues to struggling learners. Unfortunately, the rescue results in a drowning—it reinforces the students' lack of hope, robs them of a sense of mastery, and encourages learned helplessness. Unwittingly, teachers short-circuit the need to struggle and create a failure to persist because the stakes (bad grades) are too high.

The foundation of the standards-based grading paradigm is the *growth mindset*—the belief that intelligence is not fixed, but can be grown (Dweck, 2007). As teachers, once *we* embrace the mindset change and the standards-based practices that support it, we replace the enabling, rescuing, and judging with genuine support for learning. When we change *our* mindset, we change the *student's* mindset that so powerfully influences learning.

As teachers send students growth mindset messages, they demystify and redefine the process of learning. The narrative goes like this: Learning is hard and frustrating, but ultimately achievable and satisfying. Mistakes are a natural part of learning and "mistakes are something you do, not something you are" (Tough, 2012). Lack of understanding is a puzzle to be solved—not a validation of stupidity.

The supportive teacher says, "Just let me know when you are frustrated and I will help you without judging." We convince them they can succeed and we don't let them quit. We resist solving students' problems too quickly and help students "embrace struggle as a necessary part of growth" (Zmuda, 2008, p. 41).

When we release students from the stigma of failure and when we use feedback instead of grades during the process of learning, students soon develop perseverance based on the expectation of success. The teacher's support and patience for the struggle builds positive expectations and a sense of *learned optimism* in students (Seligman, 1998). Learned optimism is developed when students analyze their mistakes, figure out what they are doing wrong, and discover strategies for managing failure (Tough, 2012). As students experience mastery, they are emboldened to take control of their learning. This leads to more student self-diagnosis and self-assessment of their learning. Students' beliefs about themselves change and influence their ability to learn (Vatterott, 2007). When students believe it is possible to improve, the power of that belief is compelling. The differences in the paradigms are shown in Figure 2.3.

Figure 2.3 How Learning Is Experienced

Traditional Grading Paradigm	Results	Standards-Based Grading Paradigm	Results
• Learning is expected to be error-free—mistakes are punished	• Reinforces fixed mindset ("I'm just not smart")	• Defines learning as hard and frustrating but achievable	• Reinforces growth mindset
• Students are judged with grades while still learning	• Fear of failure	• Mistakes are a natural part of learning	• Learned optimism • Perseverance
• Failure is a judgment and a validation of ability	• Struggling students avoid learning • Teacher rescues struggling learners • Learned helplessness	• Lack of understanding is a puzzle, not a validation of stupidity • Struggle is good—BUT with support	• Students' beliefs empower them to achieve

How Grades Are Used

In the traditional grading paradigm, teachers grade everything—learning, working, and behavior. They may give or take away points for behaviors such as participation, attendance, punctuality, effort, or neatness. They may give points for work habits such as staying on task, turning in assignments on time, or completing homework. In addition, teachers may give points for extra credit work that is not related to the academic goals for the class.

For teachers who believe that rewards and punishments are *the* way to control students, grades have evolved into an elaborate system of control: Don't bring your book—10 points off; homework a day late—50 points off; talking in class—zero for the day; tardy—lose 5 points. As grades are used to punish behaviors, they overshadow the grades students receive for learning.

In the traditional grading paradigm, when teachers grade everything, the grade means nothing. When teachers combine so many things into one rating, many nonacademic factors cloud the grade—the picture becomes muddy and not reflective of learning. This practice results in two types of grade-learning mismatches. Sometimes, *high-achieving* students demonstrate mastery of content on assessments and class assignments, but receive a *low grade* because of poor behavior or because some assignments are missing or have been turned in late. Grading everything also makes it easy for *low-achieving* students to manipulate the system and mask poor academic performance. In that case, a student receives a *high grade* for the course because they are well behaved, follow rules, and have dutifully turned in all work on time, even though they show little mastery of the content (O'Connor, 2009). Their behavior has "saved" them, but a high grade without mastery of the content is no gift (Vatterott, 2009).

The Grading Game in the Traditional Grading Paradigm

The traditional grading paradigm has subverted the learning experience for both teachers and students in many subtle ways.

Traditional practices created the problem, but it did not start out that way. The question brought up by Schimmer (2013b), "When did a kindergartner ever ask 'how many points is this worth?'" is worth contemplating. Elementary students quickly learn the rules of the game we teach them. "They learn that they are supposed to finish the assignment, do it quickly and if possible get the right answer. Much more rarely does the child think he is supposed to try to understand what he is working on" (Kohn, 1993, p. 158). The grade, not learning, becomes the goal, encouraging the extrinsic motivation of reward and punishment.

What has developed is a barter system—a *quid pro quo*: "I work, you pay," with points as the currency. The teacher's weapon of control has morphed into a tool of coercion in the hands of savvy students. Grade grubbing is the norm. "What do I get for it?" is almost a form of extortion by students. Students quickly learn which actions will gain them points with each teacher—such as supplying boxes of tissues, attending the football game, or selling candy for the school fundraiser.

The results are frequent attempts at gaming the system by students and parents—whatever it takes to beat the system, including cheating (Pope, 2001). With grades rather than learning as the goal, it is not surprising that cheating is widespread. In one national survey of 36,000 secondary students, 60 percent of them admitted to cheating on tests and assignments (Strom & Strom, 2007). Shamelessly, for many students, the ends justify the means.

Other aspects of the traditional grading paradigm are equally problematic. When first attempts, including practice, are graded and when all grades are permanent, students are penalized while they are still learning. Mistakes are permanently recorded and there is no redemption (Vatterott, 2009). Add to this the practice of averaging grades, and one bad grade can seal your fate. An *F* or a zero are gifts that keep on giving and there is often no way out. A teacher once told a student who had flunked the midterm, "If you get an *A* on the final, you can get a *C* for the course." The student replied, "Yeh, like *that's* going to happen." These practices punish students for risk taking, breed a sense of hopelessness in struggling students, and often discourage them from continuing to engage in learning (Tomlinson, 2014).

Changing the Grading Game

The standards-based grading paradigm changes the game in several ways. First, only learning is graded. We use grades to report progress toward mastery of the learning standards—not behavior or working hard. Working is not rewarded with points—it is expected. Everybody works. Work habits and other non-academic behaviors, still important, are reported as a separate category on the report card. In this way, grades more accurately reflect learning, not working or compliance.

Second, there is no one-shot grading. Students are given multiple attempts after feedback to demonstrate their mastery of concepts. Instead of the extrinsic motivation of points, feedback directs learning and students experience the intrinsic motivation of progress in their learning. This moves the locus of control from the teacher to the student as learning progress replaces points. We grade in pencil—that is, new information *replaces* old information and the two are not averaged together. Instead of averaging grades, we look at patterns and evidence of learning. We assume that the latest information is the most accurate and we do not penalize students for earlier mistakes (O'Connor, 2009; Reeves, 2011). To use a sports analogy, Matt Townsley from standards-based Solon School District in Solon, Iowa, likes to say, "If you have a bad week practicing, you don't show up on Friday night with minus five on the scoreboard" (Varlas, 2013, p. 6).

In the standards-based grading paradigm, students are not penalized with grades while they are still learning. So practice, such as homework, is not graded and is used only to check for understanding and for feedback. Penalties for late work may be reflected in a work habits grade but do not affect the student's academic grade. Only the end stage of learning matters—we test for mastery of what students can demonstrate at the end of a learning sequence. Grades are deferred until the student has mastered the material. This practice makes it safe for students who do not understand concepts in the beginning of a learning cycle to continue to learn without penalty. Redemption is possible—grades can be improved with evidence of additional learning.

In the standards-based grading paradigm, there is no gaming the system by accumulating points for nonacademic behaviors—and cheating doesn't help you learn or pass the assessment. The only way to win the game is to get better at the learning. The differences in how grading is used in the two paradigms are shown in Figure 2.4.

Conclusion

To shift to a standards-based grading paradigm, we must acknowledge how traditional grading practices obstruct the learning process, damage motivation, and cause teachers and students to fixate on grades to the detriment of learning. By using what we know about learning to rethink what we do, we can change our grading methods to support rather than judge, empower learners rather than control, give choices rather than mandates, and dignify failure as an appropriate and necessary part of learning.

Standards-based grading gives a truer, more accurate picture of student learning. We can give grades that actually reflect student learning, rather than the compliance of working.

Standards-based grading requires us to let go of our grip on control and to trust students' intrinsic desire to learn. To implement the standards-based grading paradigm, we must move from a demand model, in which we use grades to control and coerce learners, to a support model, in which we provide the support necessary for learning to occur (Kohn, 1993). The teacher must become more of an advocate and less of a judge (Guskey & Bailey, 2001).

Figure 2.4 How Grades Are Used

Traditional Grading Paradigm	Results	Standards-Based Grading Paradigm	Results
• Locus of control—teacher	• Student motivation—extrinsic based on reward and punishment	• Locus of control—student	• Student motivation—intrinsic based on progress toward mastery
• Form of control—points	• Grade is the goal • *Quid pro quo*—"I work, you pay" • Gaming the system • Cheating	• Form of control—individual learning progress	• Learning is the goal • Only way to win the game is to get better at the learning • Cheating doesn't help you learn or pass the assessment
• Everything counts—grades punish behaviors such as non-completion and cheating	• Gaming the system • Grade grubbing • Grade vs. learning mismatch	• Only learning counts in the grade • Feedback directs learning • Work habits and life skills are shown as a separate category on the report card	• Grades more accurately reflect learning, not amount of work or compliance
• Grading during learning—grading homework, including late penalties	• Penalizes kids for taking risks • Breeds hopelessness	• Homework is not graded—it is used to check for understanding/provide feedback • "We don't keep score during practice"	• It's safe to make mistakes and take risks in learning
• All grades are permanent and averaged together	• One bad grade seals your fate • *F*—the gift that keeps on giving • Mistakes are permanent (no redemption)	• Test for mastery • Grade in pencil • Grades can be improved • More recent information replaces old information	• It's OK not to "get it" right away • Redemption is possible

In Chapter 3 we will explore the standards-based paradigm in action, what practices are needed for implementation, and how it affects curriculum, instruction, assessment, and the learning process.

3

What Grading Looks Like in the Standards-Based Classroom

When we move to standards-based grading, the entire process of curriculum planning, instruction, and assessment looks different. Standards drive the organization of the curriculum, which then drives daily instruction. The daily activities of the classroom look different, and the power structure changes as well, with students taking more control of how they learn. Once we understand how standards-based learning is orchestrated, we will see that the role of grading changes.

Learning Targets

To implement standards-based *grading*, we must first understand the process of standards-based *learning*. The process varies from teacher to teacher and school to school, but most begin with Common Core or other content standards established by professional associations, such as the new science standards. The standards show us the results that we want students to achieve. We then work backward from those results to create more specific learning targets. Learning targets differ from instructional objectives in that they are written in student-friendly language. "Learning targets use words, pictures, actions, or some combination of the three to express to students, in terms the students understand, the content and performance they are aiming for" (Moss & Brookhart, 2012, p. 28). They are written from the students' point of view so that students can use them to guide their learning.

We synthesize or *unpack* the standards into learning targets, usually written as "I can" or "We can" statements. Unpacking the standards into "I can" statements makes them accessible to students. Students can more clearly understand what the goal of learning is and what they must demonstrate to show they have reached the targets.

To illustrate, suppose we began our planning with two standards from the 6th grade Common Core math standards about developing an understanding of statistical variability:

- ⟩ Recognize a statistical question as one that anticipates variability in the data related to the question and accounts for it in the answers.
- ⟩ Understand that a set of data collected to answer a statistical question has a distribution which can be described by its center, spread, and overall shape. (Moss & Brookhart, 2012, p. 36)

Our instructional objectives for those standards are as follows:

- Students will explain how the element of chance leads to variability in a set of data.
- Students will represent variability using a graph. (Moss & Brookhart, 2012, p. 27)

The student-friendly learning target might read:

- ○ We will be able to see a pattern in graphs we make about the number of chips in our cookies, and we will be able to explain what made that pattern. (Moss & Brookhart, 2012, p. 39)

The 5th grade standard for opinion writing is as follows:

➘ Write opinion pieces on topics or texts, supporting a point of view with reasons and information.

Debbie Poslosky, literacy instructional coach at Craig Elementary School in Creve Coeur, Missouri, unpacked that standard into the following learning targets written in student-friendly language:

- I can introduce my topic clearly.
- I can state an opinion supported by facts and details.
- I can link opinions and reasons using phrases and clauses.
- I can provide a conclusion related to the opinion.

Eva Rudolph, 7th grade math teacher at Fox Middle School in Arnold, Missouri, began with this 7th grade math standard:

➘ Analyze proportional relationships and use them to solve real-world and mathematical problems. Recognize and represent proportional relationships between quantities.

Her learning target for students was "I can determine whether two quantities are proportional by their relationships, including real-world situations."

The standards drive learning targets, which in turn drive learning tasks. Each teacher will organize targets in a way that makes sense to them. The organization of the learning targets determines the type of learning tasks and drives how assessments will be created for those learning targets. Teachers sometimes have a tendency to create individual learning tasks for each target. But when we organize individual targets into lesson-sized tasks, teach them separately, and assess them separately, students may fail to see their relevance and connection. That method can easily become too mechanical and sterile and lead to too much direct teaching.

A better method is to group targets together so that several targets may be addressed by the same activity. Even though the teacher may be able to create separate lessons for learning targets about measurement, area, and slope, those lessons may be rote exercises using numbers without context. Instead of lesson-sized tasks, the same targets about measurement, area, and slope could be addressed with the learning task of designing a golf course. This grouping of targets allows teachers to create more engaging activities and allows students to see the bigger picture behind the standards.

Through those learning tasks, students demonstrate their level of mastery on the individual learning targets. In standards-based grading, *learning targets* drive the assessment of learning. At Craig Elementary School, one learning task for 3rd graders is to write a personal memoir. That task addresses the following 3rd grade standards:

> ⬊ Write narratives to develop real or imagined experiences or events using effective technique, descriptive details, and clear event sequences.
> b. Use dialogue and descriptions of actions, thoughts, and feelings to develop experiences and events or show the response of characters to situations.
> c. Use temporal words and phrases to signal event order.

> ⬊ Demonstrate command of the conventions of standard English capitalization, punctuation, and spelling when writing.
> c. Use commas and quotation marks in dialogue.
> e. Form and use possessives.

The rubric for the personal memoir shows the learning targets and describes the levels of mastery of each target. Figure 3.1 shows a portion of the complete rubric. Both students and teachers can use the rubric to determine progress toward proficiency of the learning targets.

Figure 3.1   Rubric for Memoir: 3rd grade

Students will write narratives to develop real or imagined experiences or events using effective techniques, descriptive details, and clear event sequences, including reflection.

Skills	Proficient	Developing	Beginning
Use a process to develop and strengthen my writing	• Produce a page or more of writing each day. • Remain engaged in a writing project for 50 to 60 minutes. • Write an entirely new draft that includes significant changes to the previous one. • Use multiple revision strategies.	• Produce at least one page of writing a day. • Remain engaged in a writing project for at least 30 minutes. • Use at least two revision strategies.	• Attempt to produce a page of writing. • Attempt to remain engaged in writing for at least 20 minutes. • With help, use a revision strategy.
Structure a memoir	• Tell the story of my life experiences bit by bit. • Write a beginning that helps the reader know the characters and setting of the event(s) in my memoir. • Use transition words such as *a little*, *later*, and *after that* to tell my memoir in order. • Write a good ending that includes action, talk, or feeling. • Write a reflection that shows how an experience changed the way I think or feel.	• Attempt to tell the story of my life bit by bit. • Attempt to write an introduction that helps the reader know the characters. • Use transition words such as *a little*, *later*, and *after that* to tell my memoir in order. • Attempt to write a good ending. • Attempt to write a reflection. • Attempt to organize memoir with paragraphs.	• Begin to tell the story of my life bit by bit. • Begin to write an introduction that helps the reader know the characters. • Begin to use transition words such as *a little*, *later*, and *after that* to tell my memoir in order. • Begin to write a good ending. • With help, begin to write a reflection. • Begin to organize memoir into paragraphs.

Figure 3.1 *(Continued)*

Skills	Proficient	Developing	Beginning
Structure a memoir—*(continued)*	• Organize memoir by using paragraphs and skipping lines to separate what happened first from what happened later.		
Develop a memoir	• Show what happened to my characters and me. • Write in a way that helps readers picture what was happening in my memoir. • Write a reflection that tells my reader why this memory is important. • Write using my voice.	• Attempt to show what happened to my characters and me. • Attempt to use descriptive words. • Attempt to write a reflection. • Attempt to use voice.	• Begin to use descriptive words. • With help, can write a reflection. • With help, is beginning to show voice.
Apply language conventions in a memoir	• Punctuate my dialogue correctly with commas and quotation marks. • Use punctuation at the end of every sentence. • Write so readers can read some parts quickly and some parts slowly. • Write so readers can read some parts in one sort of voice and others in another.	• Attempt to punctuate dialogue correctly with commas and quotation marks. • Most sentences have ending punctuation.	• Lack of punctuation interferes with readability. • With help, dialogue is beginning to be punctuated correctly.

Source: © 2014 D. Poslosky, Craig Elementary School, Creve Coeur, MO. Used by permission.

In the standards-based classroom, the learning targets are important because they are the ultimate basis for grades. We move from grading *assignments* to assessing performance and progress toward the *learning targets*. The degree to which students have reached those targets determines their final grade, *not* the number of assignments they have completed. (The specifics of determining final grades will be discussed in Chapter 4.)

Student Ownership: What Causes Learning to Happen?

As evident from the previous Common Core standard examples, today's standards and the learning targets that are created from them require students to demonstrate higher-level thinking skills. Deep thinking and application of complex knowledge cannot be taught like rote knowledge—it must be constructed in ways that are meaningful to learners (Vatterott, 2007). This brings us to the heart of the standards-based learning process—student ownership of learning. It is what *causes* learning to happen. We must take care not to become overly focused on the target and ignore the needs of individual learners.

To own their learning, students must know and understand the learning targets. This process starts with the teacher sharing the learning targets and rubrics for assessment with students and giving examples of what mastery and nonmastery of the targets look like. Teachers often give students a task that requires them to apply the targets by evaluating examples of evidence. For example, Cryslynn Billingsley, 7th grade language arts teacher at Parkway Northeast Middle School in Chesterfield, Missouri, created eight writing samples from student-submitted drafts and gave her students a rubric. Working in groups, students evaluated the writing samples and rated which samples were a 1, 2, 3, or 4 on the rubric. Then the groups defended their ratings. This activity familiarized them with the learning targets and showed them what mastery of the target looked like. It also prepared students to use the rubric later to assess their own writing.

Being aware of the targets is not enough if students are not given control over how they learn. In standards-based learning, students are full partners in their learning and work cooperatively with the teacher, a new role for everyone. Part of the ownership process begins with the teacher asking, "What learning strategies do I need to teach so they can meet the target?" and with students answering the question, "How do I learn best?" Then students must be given the freedom necessary to make decisions about their learning. In this new teacher-student partnership, teachers give students opportunities to think about their learning and to create strategies that work for them.

Jeff Harding, an algebra teacher at Mundelien High School in Mundelien, Illinois, presents the learning targets to students and then asks them, "Which way do you want to learn this?" Students choose among their textbook, video lectures, a variety of web resources, and whiteboards and get assistance as needed from the teacher. In Jeff's classroom, there is no seating chart. Students sit with peers who are working on the same target they're working on.

The ultimate realization of ownership comes when students assess their own learning. It is often more efficient than when teachers assess learning. After all, who knows the student's level of understanding better than the student? But many students have no experience in self-assessment, so they need to be taught how to assess themselves and given practice in the classroom (as Cryslynn Billingsley did with the writing samples earlier). Self-assessment is formative assessment—it should always focus on improving the student's progress toward the learning target, not on getting a better grade (Chappuis, 2009).

The more students self-assess, the more they develop ownership of their learning. As one teacher explained, "I know they are getting there when they pinpoint where they need work and they use the language of the standards." When teachers hear students say, "I need to know more about subordinating conjunctions" or "Integers are why I can't solve equations," they know students are becoming competent at self-assessment.

When students are able to self-assess their own understanding, they are empowered to take even more control over their learning. They are able to chart their progress on standards, conduct student-led conferences to demonstrate their learning, and set their own goals for improvement. Even very young students can be empowered by tracking their progress. Ashley Brumbaugh, a kindergarten teacher at Rock Island Academy in Rock Island, Illinois, has her kindergarten students create data folders with graphs showing their progress month by month on the number of sight words, letters, and numbers they know and their mastery of math targets.

Eva Rudolph's 7th grade math students track their progress on 23 math learning targets for their first semester, such as "I can multiply and divide integers" and "I can solve multistep equations." Her students take two math concept quizzes a week, each covering six learning targets. Each time they take a quiz, they record their score (0–4) on the individual learning targets. Once they have earned 4s for a specific learning target on two different quizzes, they mark out that target, and they no longer have to answer those questions on future quizzes. Toward the end of the semester, they pick their three weakest learning targets and choose a project to complete that will deepen their understanding of these concepts.

Designing Student-Focused Learning Tasks

For students to remain engaged about reaching the learning targets, learning experiences must be conducive to complex learning. It's hard to get excited about worksheets or rows of math problems. Traditional teacher-focused learning, where all decisions are made by the teacher and instruction is most often delivered as direct instruction, may not yield the results we need. Student-focused learning experiences, where students are actively engaged in learning and have choices, are much more likely to lead to the higher-order thinking skills and depth of knowledge that today's standards require (Vatterott, 2007; Wiggins & McTighe, 2005).

With student-focused learning, the primary action of the classroom becomes not the teacher's delivery of inert content but the interaction of the students with the content (Vatterott, 2007). Learning is not so much *instruction* or a *lesson* to be taught, as an *activity to be experienced*. Enthusiasm is more likely to be ignited when we design learning tasks that allow for student choice, relevance, and personalization, and tasks that "invite curiosity, interest, and engagement" (Brooks & Dietz, 2012, p. 66). As a teacher once said, "I never heard of a student not doing *his* work; it's *our* work he's not doing" (Vatterott, 2009, p. 103).

Because today's standards require application, we must do so, too—in the learning process as well as in the demonstration of learning. The best learning activities require students to demonstrate the target that you want to assess. Eva Rudolph uses a restaurant activity for students to apply computation skills and convert fractions to decimals. They use restaurant menus and coupons to order, apply the coupon, and determine the tip. Third graders at Craig Elementary School in Creve Coeur, Missouri, are asked to write book reviews (see Figure 3.2) to address this Common Core standard:

↘ Write opinion pieces on topics or texts, supporting a point of view with reasons.

In student-focused learning, the bulk of time is spent with students working independently or in groups with the teacher as the guide on the side. Of course, some direct instruction may be needed, but it should be limited to minilessons—short direct instruction lessons followed by a task that checks for understanding. Direct teaching is limited to free the teacher to be that guide and to be able to give individualized feedback. (More about how to do this in Chapter 4.)

Figure 3.2   Which Book Is Better?

Great news! Because of your outstanding reputation as an avid reader and conversationalist about books, *Best Read* magazine has asked you to review two books of your choice. Please name the books, discuss the content, and whether or not you liked the book based on the characters, plot, setting, and themes. Give evidence for your opinions and then give a recommendation for other children your age. You may use the five star approach or thumbs up, thumbs down approach. Again, we thank you for your expertise and know many authors will be anxiously awaiting your opinions!

Sincerely,
Ima Reader, Editor in Chief
Best Read magazine

Source: © 2015 D. Poslosky, Craig Elementary School, Creve Coeur, MO. Used by permission.

At Fox Middle School in Arnold, Missouri, Eva Rudolph checks for understanding by having her 7th grade math students keep interactive journals. After taking the concept quiz on the associative property in class (a formative assessment), the students write the goal "I can use properties to write equivalent equations" on the left side of their notebook page. Then on the right side of the page, students glue their class notes, often taken as foldables. The foldables serve as interactive graphic organizers and allow students to create flaps that reveal their notes about a specific topic. Then for homework they complete the "What I learned" section on the left side and create a proof to demonstrate their understanding: $5 + (7+3) = (5+7) + 3$. The "What I learned" section and the proof the student creates allows the teacher to do a quick visual check for understanding.

Ideally, when the learning experience is successful, the result is a product that can be assessed to determine if learning took place. When Tracy LaRose's 7th grade science students create calendars or mobiles to show they understand the phases of the moon, they must do research to complete the project. The *result* of the successful completion of the activity—the product—serves as the evidence of learning.

Activities can also be a way for students to apply skills they have already learned. Eva Rudolph's 7th grade math students design a Middle School of the Future—see Figure 3.3 for more information. The project requires them to apply their knowledge of the following learning targets: area and perimeter of polygons, area and perimeter of circles, and proportions and scale drawings. Those learning targets are assessed by evaluating the various aspects of the project.

Figure 3.3　Middle School of The Future—Project Outline

Campus site plan—How the site will be developed. It shows what you would see if you flew over the site, like a view from Google Earth.

School floor plan—Shows the outline of each building and location of interior walls, exits, and windows, drawn to scale.

Classroom scale model—Represents a typical classroom, drawn to scale.

Perspective drawing—A 3-D drawing of what the campus looks like.

Cost analysis of the school—The cost estimate is the total project cost for developing the site, including construction of buildings and creation of athletic fields.

Source: © 2014 Eva Rudolph, Fox Middle School in Arnold, MO. Used by permission.

Nonpunitive Feedback

If we expect students to take ownership of their learning, we must accept the fact that learning is not error-free—mistakes *will* be made during learning. If we want to encourage students to view mistakes as a necessary step in learning, we need to remove the threat of grading while they are learning. Rather than grading first attempts as we have done in traditional grading, we instead give feedback that is informative and nonjudgmental. To use a movie-making analogy, learning doesn't happen "in one take." Just as the director gives the actor feedback until he gets the performance he is satisfied with, we too continue to give supportive feedback until we get the performance we want.

When Cryslynn Billingsley at Parkway Northeast Middle School introduced complex sentences to her 7th graders, they panicked. So she created a set of notes that included definitions of complex sentences and independent, dependent, and subordinate clauses, all with examples in context. As students read the notes, they put a check mark by what they understood, put a question mark by what they "maybe understood," and circled or highlighted parts that were completely foreign to them (Vatterott, 2014). This student self-assessment served as her pre-test. The next day, Cryslynn used that information to group students based on their level of understanding for differentiated instruction. She then gave students specific learning tasks based on which concepts they needed help with. She gave a series of homework assignments on complex sentences and gave feedback until she felt students had mastered the concept. There was no grade for any of these tasks; the tasks were all used as formative feedback to the teacher and student about their level of understanding and created opportunities to practice and learn the material for the summative assessment.

Teachers have choices. We can stop grading everything students do. Learning tasks can be graded, monitored, or given feedback without grades. Grades are not necessary for learning, but feedback is. In fact, feedback has been shown to be one of the most effective strategies to improve learning (Hattie, 2009). Student progress and mastery are driven by nonpunitive feedback.

When we stop grading everything, we have more time! We can now redirect time and energy to creating learning activities and giving feedback to individual students. In the standards-based classroom, we still evaluate learning, but ungraded formative feedback replaces grading during the learning process. Feedback reoccurs throughout the sequence of learning, sometimes several times, and it may come from the teacher or peers, or it may be in the form of self-feedback.

In Tracy LaRose's 7th grade science class at Fox Middle School, students have several choices of projects, such as calendars or mobiles, that they can complete to show they understand the phases of the moon. When they think they are ready to turn in their project, Tracy does a quick visual formative assessment. If it doesn't demonstrate mastery of the required knowledge, Tracy may say, "Your answer on this part is a *3*. Go back and look at page 22," or "The phases are not in the right position. Go back and check your notes." Sometimes she asks questions like, "Why did you put the moon there?" Depending on their answers, she directs them to specific resources to help them improve their understanding so they can revise the project. Her feedback is done verbally and without grades.

In the standards-based classroom, formative feedback is nonpunitive and may or may not be recorded, but the only way it remains nonpunitive is if it is ungraded. If we must put grades in the gradebook to satisfy parents or policy, there is a way to "grade" formative feedback. When is a grade on formative feedback not a grade? When it is temporary and coded as a "no-count." As a way of monitoring progress, some teachers *do* assign a number to their feedback and record it, but give it zero weight and allow the number to be replaced when mastery is demonstrated. Grades are deferred and only used to reflect summative assessments of learning. (How and when to use grades will be discussed in Chapter 4.)

Formative feedback is part of a larger process of assessment. In standards-based grading, assessment is not an event but a process. Schimmer (2012) calls it *infused assessment*. Assessment, not grading, permeates the learning process, from pre-assessment *before* learning to determine what students already know and can do, to formative feedback *during* learning—just enough, just in time, only what the student needs (Brookhart, 2008). We shift from assessment *of learning* primarily at the *end* of a learning sequence to a continuous monitoring of progress—formative assessment *for learning* and summative assessment *of learning*. When students understand that learning is a process that occurs over time and each task is not a final assessment of learning, feedback becomes a two-way conversation between student and teacher. Formative ungraded tasks give feedback to the teacher about needed adjustments in the instructional approach. But ungraded tasks also provide an opportunity for the student to think about and talk about his or her learning and for the teacher to get inside the head of the student. In that conversation, teachers can assure students, "You just don't know it *yet*."

When 5th graders at Craig Elementary School write short stories for homework, they use an interactive checklist to communicate with their teacher and to track their progress toward meeting the Common Core standard:

> ⤷ Write narratives to develop real or imagined experiences or events using effective technique, descriptive details, and clear event sequences.

For each component skill on the checklist (e.g., "I include dialogue that is meaningful and shows responses of characters to situations"), they either state evidence that they have demonstrated the skill or explain why they have not yet achieved that part of the standard. To make assessment easier for the teacher, students also highlight the part of their short story that provides evidence. Each time they submit their short story for assessment, they use a different highlighter color so the teacher can identify the latest evidence. This system makes for an efficient conversation between student and teacher. The interactive checklist can serve multiple purposes: it can be used for student self-assessment, formative and summative assessment, student goal setting, and student-led conferences.

Conclusion

When we share learning targets with students, we give them the power to control their own learning. When we create student-focused learning activities, we spark enthusiasm for learning and we make the journey worth taking. When recurring, nonthreatening feedback replaces grading, we empower students to reach their learning goals. This is what the standards-based classroom looks like. The standards-based grading strategies needed to maximize learning in this environment will be discussed in Chapter 4.

4

What, How, and When to Grade

In Chapter 3 the concepts of infused assessment and nonpunitive feedback were introduced. But how are those concepts actually implemented day-to-day in a classroom? How do we move from points to performance—from "Does it count?" to "How will this help me learn?"

To answer that question, we need to explore what to grade or not grade, how to grade, and when to grade.

Pregrading: Things to Do Before You Grade

In the standards-based classroom, a lot of activity happens before we grade *anything*. We begin by determining a baseline of knowledge and skills for each student. Then we identify their individual learning needs and gain insight into how they learn best, and finally we customize instruction to maximize success.

Pre-testing

As assessment is infused throughout the learning process, we begin with pre-testing that assesses where students are in relation to the learning targets. Pre-tests set the stage, shape instruction for all, and guide individual learning. Pre-tests save time—once teachers know where students are in their skills or knowledge, they can plan instruction more efficiently. For instance, at Mundelein High School in Mundelein, Illinois, Jeff Harding uses a pre-test in his math classes to check for precursory skills necessary to master the course content. Students who have skills gaps then complete refresher tasks to show they are ready before they approach the learning targets for the course. Another method of pre-testing is to simply give students a checklist of the "I can" statements for the upcoming learning targets, and have them self-assess their background knowledge (Schimmer, 2012). After the pre-testing process, formative assessment provides feedback to students while they are still learning; summative assessments show the level of mastery at the end of a learning cycle.

At this point it may be helpful to clarify the use of the term *formative assessment* and to define the difference between it and *feedback*. Both can provide information to the student and the teacher about student understanding. In the previous chapters, the term *formative assessment* was used generally to describe any method of giving feedback to students about their learning while there was still time to improve. Many experts would agree that all such feedback is considered formative assessment. But the term *assessment* has been so drilled into our head as being a task or a test, that for many teachers it is confusing to call all feedback *from* students and *to* students formative assessment. Most teachers view informal feedback and formative assessment as two different things. They don't consider the actions of checking for understanding or helping students correct mistakes as formative *assessment*—it's just good teaching. It's easier to think of *formative assessment* as structured tasks designed by the teacher, the results of which may be marked or documented in some fashion, so students and parents can have a record of the student's progress toward the learning targets.

Feedback to and from Students

Feedback is a two-way recurring conversation between teacher and student. Teachers give feedback *to* students about their learning to show them where they are, but the teacher also receives feedback *from* students that allows the teacher to adjust instruction. Tomlinson (2014) sees it as "an ongoing exchange between a teacher and his or her students designed to help students grow as vigorously as possible and to help teachers contribute to that growth as fully as possible" (p. 11).

Teachers solicit feedback *from* students in several ways. All student response systems (Wiliam, 2007) allow the teacher to quickly receive feedback from the entire class. Dry erase boards or clickers enable all students to answer a question simultaneously. *Traffic lighting* allows students to signal their level of understanding of a concept by holding up a colored circle: green means "I understand," yellow means "I'm not sure," and red means "I do not understand" (Wiliam, 2007). Another method of providing this feedback is with a simple thumbs up, thumbs sideways, thumbs down (Tomlinson, 2014). Students may also respond to multiple-choice questions by voting with their fingers (one finger signals the correct answer is A; two fingers is B).

Teachers may receive feedback from individual students through student journaling, during class, or as homework. Math teacher Jeff Harding uses journaling at the end of the class period in this way:

> Students are asked to write a summary of the things that struck them about the class that day. This could be something new they learned or something they want to be sure to remember—whatever they felt was critical to the day's class. This whole process takes about five minutes. Sometimes this shows me that further clarification is needed, while other times I take note of something really good that they said to share with the rest of the class. Listening to them has been a clear and quick way for me to assess their understanding of the concept.

Informal feedback *to* students might include verbal redirection, perhaps by asking questions or clarifying a task. For teachers to be able to give feedback to students, it is necessary to limit direct instruction and to create activity-based lessons. As discussed in Chapter 3, these strategies free the teacher to work individually with students, to spot-check student progress, and to guide them in the right direction.

Jim Drier, language arts teacher at Mundelein High School in Mundelein, Illinois, uses Socratic-style seminars, discussions, and individual conversations to give students feedback. Cryslynn Billingsley, language arts teacher at Parkway Northeast Middle School in Creve Coeur, Missouri, uses a clipboard during her class discussions to record students' level of understanding of a topic that she can later share with individual students.

All feedback does not have to come from the teacher; peer feedback can also be useful. In Cryslynn Billingsley's language arts class, students are given a question such as "How would you format a theme analysis response?" Students put their answers on sticky notes, exchange them, and help each other fill in what's missing. Peers help each other check their own understanding.

Here's another peer feedback strategy:

> Before students can turn in an assignment, they must trade papers with a peer. Each student then completes a "pre-flight checklist" by comparing the peer's document against a list of required elements. For example, the pre-flight checklist for a lab report might require, among other things, a title, a date, diagrams drawn in pencil and labeled, and results that are clearly separated from conclusions. Only when the peer has signed off on the checklist can the work be turned in to the teacher. (Wiliam, 2007, p. 194).

Differentiation

Differentiation is embedded in the process of standards-based learning—not only is time varied from one student to the next but the methods of learning and demonstrating learning are varied. As we give targeted feedback to individual students and as they are empowered to learn in their own way, the differences in learners become smaller. The more students self-assess how they learn best, the more students create their own differentiations. If, after repeated attempts, a student or group of students has failed to master a learning target, we must take a fearless inventory of our instructional process and ask ourselves these questions:

- Was their level of learning properly diagnosed with pre-testing?
- Was the feedback about learning timely, specific, and helpful?
- Did our differentiations move the student or group of students forward?

Regrouping for Reteaching

Regrouping for learning is an easy and efficient form of differentiation. Using the results of a pre-test, feedback, or formative or summative assessment, teachers can identify "patterns in the students' work" or "clusters of student need" (Tomlinson, 2014, p. 14). Students can then be organized into two or more groups for ungraded group learning. Students may be grouped by level of proficiency or by specific learning targets that they need to work on.

Cryslynn Billingsley uses the results of formative assessment to place students in one of three groups. She calls it *pack and stack day* because students pack up their belongings and move to a table with others who need practice on the same skill or concept. Pack and stack day is a good way to review information. One table might be working on an assignment to enrich or add more depth to their work because the students already have the skill or concept mastered. They may be working on how to show the work in a new way. Another table of students may be working on a scaffolding activity to improve their understanding on the pieces of the skill they may not completely understand. The last table will work directly with the teacher because they need to be retaught the information and this will allow them to learn the information in a guided way. The activities at each table are based on the errors that students made on the formative assessment. (This strategy is from Adaptive Schools/Thinking Collaborative/ Center for Cognitive Coaching.)

While students are working, Cryslynn monitors student progress with colored cups. Each student is given a red, yellow, and green cup and uses the cups to give feedback to the teacher. The yellow is "I have a quick question, but I can keep working until you get to me." The red is "I'm stuck and need you to come right away." The green is "I know exactly what I'm doing."

Another method has students self-assess their level of understanding with the "fist to five" strategy. Students rate their level of understanding by signaling with their hand. That signal determines how they will be grouped for reteaching or additional practice (Schimmer, 2013a). See Signals as Student Responses for an explanation.

Signals as Student Responses

Student Response	Suggested Next Step for Learning
0 (a fist) = "I am completely lost"	Work with teacher
1 finger = "I need a lot of help"	Work with teacher
2 fingers = "I understand it, but I need to practice more"	Work with peers
3 fingers = "I understand it, but could use some extra help"	Work with peers
4 fingers = "I feel confident that I can do it independently"	Work alone
5 fingers = "I feel like I have it mastered"	Work alone

Source: Schimmer, 2013a.

Teachers could obviously use this feedback to regroup differently, perhaps moving some groups to computer-assisted instruction, using the 4s and 5s to peer tutor 2s and 3s, or providing enrichment options for the 5s.

Often teachers simply divide students into two groups: mastery and nonmastery. Tracy LaRose's 7th graders at Fox Middle School in Arnold, Missouri, complete a Phases of the Moon Project. After a pre-test, she divides students into two groups. The members of the mastery group will work on an enrichment activity in small groups, and the members of the nonmastery/partial mastery group will work individually to complete a WebQuest and a series of diagrams for a poster. When a student in the nonmastery/partial mastery group completes his project, he moves into the mastery group.

Using regrouping as a differentiation leads to less whole-class instruction, more small groupings, more individual learning, and more computer-assisted instruction. Larger schools may choose to regroup students among instructors (for instance, three teachers all teaching the same course or the same grade level). Smaller schools may use multiage groupings. The classroom organization changes to facilitate groups of students working at different levels of mastery simultaneously.

What Not to Grade

At each step in the learning process, teachers must make decisions about what to grade or not grade. Sometimes schoolwide policies force their hand by mandating, for instance, that the final grade be comprised of 80 percent summative assessments and 20 percent formative assessments. Just as often, though, teachers have total control. In a purely standards-based grading system, only summative assessment "counts" in the final grade.

Formative Assessment

Formative assessment provides feedback about student learning prior to the summative assessment. Formative assessment should be organized by learning target and results should be reported by learning target. To be used effectively, students are expected to demonstrate the same level of skill or knowledge in the formative assessment that is expected in the summative assessment. For instance, if the summative assessment requires students to apply and analyze information, a formative assessment that only requires rote memory is inadequate and misleading. Typically formative assessments are evaluated and descriptive feedback is given to the learner, such as with practice tests.

Ungraded practice tests are especially beneficial to learners as they activate "retrieval learning" and strengthen the connections in the brain. One technique for practice tests is called "Find It and Fix It." Rather than marking the answers that are incorrect, the teacher notes to the student, "Five of these are incorrect; find them and fix them" (Wiliam, 2007). This requires the student to reengage with the questions and precipitates a lot of learning. Obviously the student would be allowed to use resources and ask the teacher for help if she is unable to either find or fix those mistakes.

Math teacher Jeff Harding uses mastery checks for formative assessment. These mastery checks are typically between 6 and 12 problems (all about one learning target) at different levels of difficulty. As Jeff explains:

> These assessments are written using three levels: green, yellow, and red. The green level questions are basic skill problems and generally require only one or two steps to solve. The yellow level questions require multiple steps and/or multiple ideas to solve. The red level questions are generally questions that the students have never seen before, requiring them to go beyond the knowledge they have obtained and/or apply the knowledge to a new situation.

The green and yellow level questions indicate student progress toward mastery of the learning target and show them how close they are to mastery. The red level questions challenge students to exceed mastery of the target. Students are expected to attempt all three levels of questions. Their answers help the teacher to determine the students' level of mastery.

Formative assessment may also be the first attempt at what will eventually be a summative assessment. First graders at Craig Elementary School in Creve Coeur, Missouri, use the reading checklist in Figure 4.1 to self-assess their nonfiction reading. This checklist assesses several learning targets. For each set of "I can" statements, students list evidence that shows they have reached the target or they check the column marked "not yet." The checklist is the same rubric that is used as the summative assessment for the same learning targets.

Figure 4.1 Navigating Nonfiction Reading Checklist: 1st Grade

---

I can do the following:	Here is my evidence:	Yes	Not Yet
Identify and describe characteristics of nonfiction.			
Ask questions to focus my learning.			
Identify key details.			
Use pictures and words to think about the text.			
Identify a variety of text features.			
Use context clues.			
Use schema.			

Source: © 2014 D. Poslosky, Craig Elementary School, Creve Coeur, MO. Used by permission.

Homework as Formative Assessment

The traditional focus of homework has been on *working*—all students have to complete all the assigned work (often low-level rote tasks) by a specified time, or risk the punishment of a low grade (Vatterott, 2009). Homework in a standards-based system is different in three ways. First, the standards have raised the bar: rote practice is out; task complexity is in. Students don't just write spelling words; they use them to write declarative essays. They don't complete 20 identical math problems; they apply math skills to new problems. Second, homework is differentiated based on student need. As students analyze the relationship between the homework they are completing and their performance on assessments, they discover the most effective tasks for them (Vatterott, 2014). Third, in a traditional classroom, students often perceived homework as busy work and typically didn't see the connection of homework to summative assessments. In a standards-based system it is *explicit*—what do you *need* to do to master the specific learning targets?

The current consensus is that homework should be formative assessment that checks for understanding or that helps prepare students for summative assessments. Therefore, in a truly standards-based system, homework should not be graded. Standards-based policies usually state that homework will be reviewed and feedback will be given, but not counted in the grade. Often completion of homework is reported separately on the report card as a work habit (Vatterott, 2010). To explain the logic of this practice to students and parents, the following statements are helpful:

- Does it count? Yes, because it helps you pass the formative or summative assessment.
- If it doesn't count, there is no motivation to cheat; the motivation is to pass the assessment.
- Accountability comes when you pass or fail the assessment (delayed gratification).

Ideally homework or any other formative assessment is not graded and does not count in the final grade, but in reality, in many schools formative assessment *does* still count in the grade. This may be a result of the tradition of grading *all* work (rewarding *working* instead of *learning*), a mistrust of students to work without grades, or even pressure from parents. Although some schools have limited the percentage that formative assessment counts in the grade, there are several reasons why counting it in the grade at all is less than desirable. "Students often feel that assessment equals test equals grade equals judgment. That association leads many discouraged students to give up rather than to risk another failure" (Tomlinson, 2014, p. 11). Grading when students are still learning sends the message that if you don't learn quickly, you must not be very smart. Counting formative assessment in the final grade is especially detrimental (not to mention misleading) when grades are averaged. The student is then penalized for a lack of mastery early in learning, even though mastery was achieved later.

When formative assessments are not counted in the final grade, teachers may "mark" formative assessments with a symbol such as a check mark, an *X* or a plus or minus sign, or with letters indicating a level of mastery such as progressing (P) or not quality yet (NQY). Some teachers give number grades, as for other assignments, but treat them as no-counts—a temporary grade that carries zero weight in determining the final grade.

It is critical that students see the relationship between feedback, formative assessment, and summative assessments as progressive. As students begin to experience feedback and formative assessment as information and not judgment, they realize that their learning can improve and that they can learn from mistakes (Guskey, 2007). To use the analogy of actors in a stage production, feedback is like a *rehearsal* for a performance with no audience present; during the rehearsal the actors get feedback on how to improve their performance. Formative assessment is more often like a *dress rehearsal*. How close can I come to getting it right? The summative assessment is the *actual performance* seen by the public. So although the dress rehearsal is not perfect, the only thing that "counts" is the final performance, and that is what receives the grade. The final achievement of learning is more important than the steps it took to get there.

What to Grade—Summative Assessments

When determining what to grade, the answer is simple. Grade only learning, and grade only the student's last best effort to demonstrate that learning. Formative assessment is assessment *for* learning and occurs when there is still time to improve. Summative assessments are assessments *of* learning that occur at the end of a predetermined learning cycle, after learning has taken place (O'Connor, 2009; Stiggins, 2007). Assessments serve to verify that learning has occurred and to report to parents and others. How an assessment is used is what determines whether it is formative or summative (Schimmer, 2012).

In a traditional classroom, summative assessments would typically be a paper-and-pencil unit test, midterm, or final exam. That assessment would be given to all students on the same day, given only one time, and the score on the assessment would be final. In the standards-based classroom, summative assessments are not limited to paper-and-pencil tests. Performance tasks such as a paper, a project, a demonstration, or a presentation may also be used. Summative assessments are often common assessments (used for all sections of a course or all students in a grade level) and are typically organized by learning targets. Assessments that cover multiple targets are reported out as separate scores by target. For instance, if a 100-point social studies test addressed three learning targets, the questions would be organized by target and three scores would be recorded in the grade book—such as 35 points possible about continuity/change, 35 points possible about principles of government, and 30 points possible about geography/culture.

Ideally, students only take the summative assessment when they feel they are ready. But some students may never feel ready! So sometimes teachers give the summative assessment to get a sense of how close students are to being ready. Sometimes when giving a summative assessment, teachers will allow students to choose a window of time, such as which day the following week they want to take the test. Concerns about students sharing what's on the test is not an issue in a standards-based system—they *know* what's going to be on the test because the formative assessment evaluated the same knowledge and skills. If we want students to be successful at summative assessments, we need to rethink the conditions under which the assessment is given.

- Do students know in advance the skills and knowledge being assessed, and have they had adequate time to prepare?
- Is adequate time provided to complete the assessment?
- What resources can the student use?
- Is the assessment a true measure of understanding or of rote memory?
- Can another task show mastery, such as a verbal test or a project?

How to Grade

The method of grading should reflect student progress toward individual learning targets. As students improve in their learning, more recent evidence should replace previous evidence. Students who eventually achieve mastery should not be penalized for earlier struggles.

Grade by Learning Target

In traditional grading, grades are recorded by the task—a grade for a particular assignment, quiz, or test. In standards-based grading, those learning tasks are organized by learning targets and grades are reported by learning target. The Rock Island–Milan School District in Rock Island, Illinois, illustrates it in this way:

Traditional Grade Book Recorded by Assignment

Name	Homework Average	Quiz 1	Chapter Test 1
Bill	50	75	78
Susan	100	50	62
Felicia	10	90	85

Source: © 2015 Rock Island–Milan School District #41, Rock Island, IL. Used by permission.

Standards-Based Grade Book Recorded by Learning Target

Name	Learning Target 1 Write an alternate ending for a story	Learning Target 2 Identify elements of a story	Learning Target 3 Compare and contrast two stories
Bill	Meeting (3)	Meeting (3)	Progressing (2)
Susan	Progressing (2)	Progressing (2)	Progressing (2)
Felicia	Exceeding (4)	Meeting (3)	Meeting (3)

Source: © 2015 Rock Island–Milan School District #41, Rock Island, IL. Used by permission.

Grade by Level of Mastery of the Target

How do we know what level of mastery a student has achieved on each learning target? The level of mastery is determined by the "I can" statements associated with that level for that target. At Clear Creek Amana Middle School in Tiffin, Iowa, all teachers use the same language for all learning targets—exceeds, secure, developing, beginning. Those levels of mastery are further clarified to students with "I can" statements (see Figure 4.2).

Figure 4.2   Descriptors for Providing Feedback to Students

- Exceeds: Ready for a challenge!
  - I can complete the task without help.
  - I can explain how to do the task in my own words.
  - I can help someone who is struggling with the task.
  - I can explain how it applies to my life.

- Secure: I got it!
  - I can complete the task without help.
  - I can show that I understand.
  - I can find my own mistakes.

- Developing: I'm getting there!
  - I can complete the task with help or an example in front of me.
  - I may still make a few mistakes.
  - I can find my mistakes with help from someone.

- Beginning: I need help!
  - I can follow the task while someone explains it to me.
  - I cannot figure out what I am doing wrong.
  - I cannot figure out how to start.

Source: © 2015 Clear Creek Amana Middle School, Tiffin, IA. Used by permission.

Grade in Pencil

At a conference in Baltimore, Maryland, Robert Canady said, "What's ruining education is ink," referring to our tendency to make all grades permanent. He also said that the goal of standards-based learning is mastery and students may need more than one attempt to get there (2010).

> If students demonstrate that past assessment information no longer accurately reflects their learning, that information must be dropped and replaced by the new information. Continuing to rely on past assessment data miscommunicates students' learning. (Guskey, 1996, p. 21)

The most recent evidence of learning is the most accurate and grades should be replaced by the most recent evidence (O'Connor, 2009; Reeves, 2011). Drivers are not restricted by how many times they took the driver's test and their scores are not averaged together. A lawyer's license to practice law does not indicate how many times he or she took the bar exam. To quote assessment guru Tom Schimmer at a conference in Portland, Oregon, "School is the only place where it *matters,* that I didn't know something *before* that I know *now*" (2013b).

Adapting Standards-Based Grading for a Letter or Percentage System

A high school teacher once asked, "Why go to all the trouble of doing standards-based grading if you're just going to convert it to a letter anyway?" In a perfect world, standards-based grades would be the norm and letter grades and percentages would be a thing of the past. This is already happening in many elementary and middle schools across the United States. Elementary and middle schools can easily use descriptors such as proficient, developing, or advanced to label students' progress toward mastery. Numbers or letters are unnecessary at those levels since grades do not need to be communicated beyond parents or the school. However, most high schools using standards-based grading feel the need to convert descriptors to numbers that can eventually be converted to letter grades. Even if such a conversion is necessary, standards-based grades still give us a more accurate picture of what students know and can do than traditional grades. There are a variety of methods for using standards-based grading while operating in a traditional letter grade system.

Some schools still use percentages but report them by learning target. For example, at Nisqually Middle School in Lacey, Washington, all math teachers report grades by learning target. The final exam is the last opportunity to improve scores on individual learning targets. Final exams are organized and scored by learning target and will count as a retest. These scores will replace any *lower* grade book entries, but no entries already in the grade book will be lowered by the results of the final exam. Nisqually Middle

School's letter explaining their policy to parents is shown in the Appendix (p. 112). Figure 4.3 is an excerpt of what three students' grades at Nisqually Middle School might look like.

Figure 4.3 Excerpt from Grade Book: 8th Grade Math

Student	Solve Equations 8.EE.7	Graph Linear Equations 8.F.4	Scatter Plots for Bivariate Data 8.SP.1	Apply Laws of Exponents 8.EE.1	FINAL GRADE
Patrick	80	80	80	80	80 (*B-*)
Jack	40	50	90	100	70 (*C-*)
Anne	90	90	100	20	75 (*C*)

Source: © 2015 Forrest Clark, Nisqually Middle School, Lacey, WA. Used by permission.

Even after the final exam, Jack failed to master two learning targets and Anne failed to master one. The policy at Nisqually Middle School states that students' grades are percentages for each standard and that their final grade is the average of those percentages. But the policy gives individual teachers the option to choose to average by median, mean, or mode and the option to exclude a low score.

Adapting a *0–4* Grading System

Some teachers who have moved to a *0–4* grading system are still required to report grades as letters or percentages. Teachers use different methods of conversion, each yielding slightly different results. Here are a few examples.

As shown earlier in the chapter, all teachers at Clear Creek Amana Middle School in Tiffin, Iowa, use the same descriptors to give feedback to their students. The descriptors are recorded in the grade book as numbers that translate into percentages and letter grades—see Figure 4.4. A complete copy of the Clear Creek Amana's Guidelines for Grading is in the Appendix (p. 109).

Figure 4.4   Grading Rubric: Middle School

Statement	Rubric Number	Percentage	Grade	Comment
Exceeds	4	100	A	• I can complete the task without help. • I can explain how to do the task in my own words. • I can help someone who is struggling with the task. • I can explain how it applies to my life.
Secure	3.5	87.5	B	• I can complete the task without help. • I can show that I understand. • I can find my own mistakes.
Developing	3	75	C	• I can complete the task with help or an example in front of me. • I may still make a few mistakes. • I can find my mistakes with help from someone.
Beginning	2	50	F Not Acceptable	• I can follow the task while someone explains it to me. • I cannot figure out what I am doing wrong. • I cannot figure out how to start.

Source: © 2015 Clear Creek Amana Middle School, Tiffin, IA. Used by permission.

Lynette Fast, art specialist at Lincoln North Star High School in Nebraska, scores all assignments *0–4* using the following rubrics:

0 = No attempt or not present

1 = Emerging/some understanding

2 = Comprehension level

3 = Application level

4 = Highly proficient—synthesis/able to reflect, etc.

Students complete multiple tasks for each learning target. Then all evidence for each target is averaged together to give one score for each target. All targets are weighted equally, and the averages for each target are averaged together for the final grade. Here is how Lynette computed Joe's grade (LT = learning target):

Excerpt from a Standards-Based Grade Book

	LT 1 Task 1	LT 1 Task 2	LT 1 Task 3	Average LT 1
Joe	2	3	3	2.67

	LT 2 Task 1	LT 2 Task 2	Average LT 2	
Joe	4	4	4	

	LT 3 Task 1	LT 3 Task 2	Average LT 3	QUARTER AVERAGE
Joe	3	2	2.5	3.05

When Lynette began using this system, she still had to convert her *0–4* numbers to percentages and letter grades for her district's report card. She worked with the central office fine arts coordinator to set values within the district's computerized grading system that would automatically convert the *0–4* numbers to percentages for the final grade calculation. Together they decided how each number would convert to percentages:

1 = 65%

2 = 75%

3 = 85%

4 = 95%

On a 100-point scale:

> 90–100 = *A*
> 80–89 = *B*
> 70–79 = *C*
> 60–69 = *D*

With Lynette's system, Joe would earn a *B*. In other districts, they may choose to use the percentage of total points earned. A total of 28 points are possible (seven tasks each with 4 points possible). By this method, Joe earned a total of 21 out of 28 points, giving him a 75 percent or a *C*.

Although standards-based grading purists cringe at the thought ("A *3* is not a *B*!"), many school systems have found some form of a conversion a palatable compromise when transitioning to a standards-based reporting system. But that conversion is not an easy process—a point of contention emerges when teachers must convert *3*s and *4*s to letter grades. Many schools have written their descriptors in such a way that a *3* equals *meeting* the standard and to earn a *4*, the student must *exceed* the standard. This is not a problem if the number does not have to be converted to a letter, as is often the case in elementary and middle schools. But most standards-based high schools convert the *0–4* scale to a letter grade. The question then becomes "What letter grade *is* representative of mastery?" Some would say if the student has met the standard, their grade should be an *A*. But if the school converts a *3* to a *B* and a *4* to an *A*, then the student who *meets* the standard gets a *B*, and only the student who *exceeds* the standard can get an *A*. In that case, some people would argue that makes the *4* (*exceeds*) the real standard for mastery. One alternative suggested by Jeff Harding at Mundelein High School in Mundelein, Illinois, would be to allow "meets" to be an *A* and "exceeds" to be given honors credit. Schools use a variety of complex formulas, such as this one suggested by Reeves (2011, p. 66):

A = At least four assessments with a final score of 4 and two assessments with a final score of at least 3.

B = At least four assessments with a final score of at least 3 and two assessments with a final score of at least 2.

C = At least three assessments with a final score of at least 3.

When to Grade

Decisions about when to grade should be based on when we believe the student has reached the learning target. Some students will need more time, more attempts, and more remediation than others.

How Do I Handle Retakes?

A better question might be "How do I make sure students are ready for assessments?" A general axiom might be "more pre-test/less retest." If learning targets are clearly articulated and adequate feedback is being provided, there should be fewer retakes needed on formative and summative assessments. Schools and teachers vary in their policies regarding retakes. Some teachers allow students to retake formative assessments but not summative assessments, while some allow retakes on summative assessments but not formatives, and some allow retakes on both. Ideally, there should be a schoolwide policy.

What seems to make sense is to have more and better formative assessments. If those assessments give accurate feedback to learners on how to reach the target and students are allowed to retake formative assessments until they master the learning, students shouldn't need to retake summative assessments. If, for instance, students couldn't take the summative assessment until they had passed three formative assessments on that target, retakes on the summative assessment would be rare. In Jeff Harding's algebra class, summative assessments (quizzes) count for

100 percent of the grade. They are learning target specific and may be retaken as many times as needed after proven remediation (see the following section on Hoops). Summative assessments are the common assessments given by all algebra teachers in the building.

Retakes are typically limited to only the targets the student hasn't mastered and may be optional or mandatory. For example, in Forrest Clark's math class at Nisqually Middle School in Lacey, Washington, students who score below 80 percent on a specific learning target are required to reassess. Mandatory retake "floors" (such as 70 percent or 80 percent) must also come with an optional "ceiling." If some students are *required* to retake to raise their score, students who score above the floor must be *allowed* the option to retake, even if their score is 95 percent.

One thing is becoming apparent—there are no free retakes. Students should never be allowed to retest without showing additional evidence that they have mastered the concepts that caused them to do poorly on the original assessment. As one principal said, "Kids will reassess blindly." Retakes without remediation is an exercise in futility and frustration for both the student and the teacher.

Hoops

Teachers design a variety of "hoops" or remediations that students must complete in order to qualify for a retake. Often reteaching is prescribed or students must complete additional work, such as study guides, computer-assisted instruction modules, WebQuests, or instructional videos. Sometimes what is needed is a scaffolding tool such as a graphic organizer or concept map. These remediations must be chosen carefully; there must be evidence that the hoop is actually effective in improving the student's progress toward the target. For many teachers, discovering effective hoops will be a process of trial and error. Remember that our goal is to minimize the number of retakes a student needs to show mastery.

One common hoop is to have students correct their errors on a failed assessment. But test corrections are often ineffective; they may help the student see what he or she did wrong on the test, but they don't necessarily improve his or her understanding or command of the content. If test corrections are used, a format is needed that causes students to analyze whether their incorrect answers were simple mistakes, misconceptions, or a lack of understanding of the concepts. Additional tasks beyond the test correction may be required.

Another common hoop for retakes is that "Students must complete all practice that was assigned." Often this hoop is aimed at students who did not complete homework. If lack of practice is truly the reason the student failed the assessment, this may work. It may not be effective if the student didn't understand the practice the first time around or if the practice is not consistent with the performance expected on the assessment. "Complete all missing homework" should be a hoop only if the teacher is confident that doing so will truly remediate the student's understanding. We want the hoops to result in additional learning, not just force students to complete missing work.

Jeff Harding's students who don't demonstrate mastery on a summative assessment can take a reassessment only after completing a reassessment ticket. On that form they document what steps they have taken to prepare for the reassessment, such as tutoring, doing additional work, or demonstrating the target. See Figure 4.5 for a copy of the reassessment ticket.

The consensus of standards-based practitioners is that retakes are *replacement scores*. They are not averaged with the old score and there is no grade penalty for retaking (e.g., "You can't get higher than a *B* on the retake"). But what if the retake score is *lower* than the previous score? There are two schools of thought here. Some teachers count it as practice and don't record it ("do no harm"). Other teachers replace the earlier score with the retake score, even though it is lower. This second option "ups

---

Figure 4.5   Reassessment Ticket

Name _____ Today's Date _____

Instructional Objective _____

What steps have you taken to be prepared for a reassessment?

Evidence (such as additional notes or extra problems) must be attached.

Check all that apply

☐ FAST tutoring

☐ Additional practice problems

☐ Met with teacher or tutor

☐ Written summary (explain everything you did wrong and create/solve
   similar problems correctly

Date and time I would like to reassess _____

Source: © 2014 Jeff Harding. Adapted by permission.

the stakes" on the retake—it may discourage students from reassessing, but it may also lead to more reassessments as students struggle to regain their previous score. (Issues of logistics and the scheduling of retakes will be discussed in Chapter 5).

Conclusion

The key action in the standards-based classroom is not grading but feedback, with students looping back for remediation when needed. Feedback is *free help*—there is no grade or mark associated with feedback. Formative assessments give students multiple opportunities to improve, free from the threat of grades while they are still learning, and summative assessments verify and report their learning progress.

For students who learn quickly, teachers can enrich and extend their learning. For students who struggle, teachers create new paths for learning and change remedies that aren't working. When we acknowledge and respect differences in learners, we adjust our classroom routine to make success possible for all students. Chapter 5 will outline the systemic changes needed to fully support standards-based learning.

5

How to Reform Grading: Making Change Happen

In Chapter 2 the paradigm shift from traditional grading to standards-based grading was outlined. It offered a comprehensive shift in how learning is defined, structured, and experienced, as well as how grades are used. But meaningful grading reform can happen without implementing all aspects of the paradigm at once. Changes need not be grandiose to have a huge effect on student learning or to improve the accuracy and validity of student grades. Change can start with one teacher, a team of teachers, or an entire school faculty or school district. In many classrooms and schools, small changes are easier to accomplish.

Defining Purpose

Whether the scale of change in grading practices begins with an individual teacher, a team, or a faculty, awareness of the *purpose* of grades must come first. We must decide what we believe about the purpose of grading. That decision-making process will reveal that grading reform is about more than just grading:

> What many schools find as they try to establish purpose for their grading system is that they have to deal with teachers' beliefs and long-standing habits and experience, not only about grading but also about learning, effort, discipline, and classroom management. (Brookhart, 2011, p. 12)

Our belief in the purpose of grading is the foundation that makes our practices defensible to students, parents, and community.

Aligning Practice to Purpose

Our purpose guides our decisions about grading practices. We may ask ourselves, "Based on what I believe to be the purpose of grading, what should count in the grade? What should not count in the grade?" Decisions about "what counts" may include formative assessment, group work, extra credit, homework, and behaviors such as participation, tardiness, and cheating.

For an individual teacher, existing school policy may restrict some of these decisions, but quite often there is no formal policy about grading. In that case, teachers may have total freedom in how and what they grade. On the other hand, schools that implement standards-based grading often have more prescriptive guidelines that address many of the issues regarding what does and does not count in the grade. Standards-based schools have typically removed all nonacademic behaviors from the grade. If they believe the purpose of grading is to accurately reflect achievement, then it becomes inconsistent to punish behaviors such as cheating, tardiness, or attendance with grades. Some schools count only summatives in the grade, and some limit grading to formative and summative assessments. Those schools usually specify the weighting of formative and summative assessments. (A commonly used formula is 20 percent for formatives and 80 percent for summatives.) Many schools limit the percentage homework may count in the grade, some consider homework as part of formative assessment, and others do not allow homework to count in the grade at all.

Even within detailed grading policies, teachers usually still retain considerable freedom to align their practices with their beliefs. For instance, there may be a policy that homework must count for a certain percentage of the grade, but there may be no stipulation about penalties for missing or late work, for differentiating the type or amount of homework, or about homework being completed in class. If an individual teacher believes the purpose of grading is to reflect academic achievement only, they could begin by removing nonacademic behaviors from the grade, by no longer grading practice work, and by giving more ungraded formative feedback. The important thing is that to the greatest extent possible, our practices should be consistent with and faithful to our beliefs about the purpose of grading.

Aligning Practice to Purpose as a Team or School

As teachers, we may be working alone with little support to change grading practices in our classroom. In the beginning we may not have the consensus of others, but what one teacher starts can grow into a larger movement as others see the results and begin working toward the same goal. When we agree on the purpose of grading as a team, department, or school faculty, our beliefs help us find common ground—they unite us as a group. Working as a grade-level team or department brings more options and flexibility, and working as a building faculty allows for even more organizational changes that can support standards-based practices. When we agree on purpose, methods follow purpose (Guskey, 2015).

If we are attempting to change practices at the grade level, department, or school level, there are additional challenges and opportunities in aligning practice to purpose. Groups must be sensitive to balancing teacher freedom with a need for consistency across teachers within a department or grade level. Teachers at Minnetonka High School in Minnetonka, Minnesota, chose accuracy and consistency as their values for their grading system. To reinforce their commitment to consistency, the school makes students a promise that no matter which teacher they have, they will be graded the same way. Working together, groups need to reach consensus on which practices should be standardized as common policy and which practices will be individual teacher choice. Other decisions may include the following:

- Can we remove some or all student behaviors from the grade? If not totally, can we limit them to a small part of the grade?
- If we remove behaviors from the academic grade, how else can we monitor and report behaviors that are important to us? Should we create a separate work habits category or citizenship mark?
- What systems, indicators, and increments will be used to report grades—letters, percentages, or a *0–4* scale?

Adapting Organizational Practices and Policies

Many aspects of traditional school organization, such as grouping students by grade level, credit based on seat-time, and traditional course scheduling, can limit our efforts to implement standards-based grading (DeLorenzo et al., 2009). So although we can begin to make changes at the classroom level, there are many organizational practices at the building level that can enhance our efforts. Buildingwide implementation of standards-based grading is easier when there is systemic support. With organizational changes, we can optimize learning conditions and more efficiently implement standards-based grading. Standards-based grading can be supported through changes in schedules and use of time, use of personnel, and changes in policy.

Changes in Schedules or Use of Time

Standards-based grading requires time. For students, changes in the schedule can accommodate differences in learning style and speed of learning, and can allow students to be regrouped as needed. Creative scheduling can also give teachers the freedom to share students for reteaching. For instance, in a large high school, the master schedule may be altered so that all Algebra I sections are taught during 1st and 6th hour. With multiple teachers teaching the same course at the same time, teachers can work together to regroup students for reteaching on specific concepts. Similarly, elementary teachers can coordinate schedules to regroup 3rd graders for reteaching or even regroup students across grade levels as needed. Strategic scheduling makes the logistics of retakes and reteaching easier by building academic lab or intervention periods into the school day.

Schedules can also serve a proactive function by catching students before they need remediation. East Union Elementary School in Afton, Iowa, uses a schedule of 40-minute blocks to prioritize literacy and math. Since both 1st grade teachers have the same schedule, they can regroup students across the two classrooms. The schedule in Figure 5.1 (p. 87) has also been arranged so that for two blocks of time each day, the special education teacher can work with students with special needs and the Title I teacher can work with students who need Tier 3 interventions.

At Forest Grove High School in Forest Grove, Oregon, a school with a 50 percent Latino population and more than 50 percent free and reduced lunch population, all 9th graders who are in danger of not meeting the state benchmarks in reading and/or math are enrolled in a mandatory reading workshop and a mandatory math workshop to identify and remediate deficiencies. Over several years, student reading proficiency has improved from 50 percent to 76 percent and student math proficiency has improved from 33 percent to 83 percent. The number of graduates who were college bound rose from 40 percent to 70 percent. Their eight-block freshman schedule (four academic courses each day) looks like this:

Block 1   Math
Block 2   Science
Block 3   Language arts
Block 4   Social studies
Block 5   Math workshop
Block 6   Reading workshop
Block 7   Health
Block 8   Elective

At North Middle School in Rapid City, South Dakota, all students have a 50-minute regular math class and about half receive an additional 50-minute math intervention class. Based on data, students are placed in one of three math interventions. Option 1 is Math Lab, for students who are at most one to two grade levels behind. In this intervention setting, students spend 2½ class periods a week in focused acceleration (front-loading the next concepts to be learned), two days in focused remediation to fill in gaps in skills, and a half day a week working on any missing tests or assignments. Option 2 is Math 180, for students who are two to four grade levels below. They work strictly on remediation. Option 3 uses a one-to-four teacher-student ratio to provide intensive help. At the end of each semester, students are reevaluated and may be moved to a different intervention option. For instance, students moving out of Math 180 automatically go into Math Lab. These classes are intended to be fluid, so if a student proves to be proficient at any time in the semester, he or she can exit Math Lab. Students who are on grade level for math may take an elective class in place of math intervention or accelerated math in place of a regular math class.

East Union Secondary School in Afton, Iowa, has had success with a four-block schedule. Students take four full-year courses each semester, giving them fewer subjects to juggle. Language and math are taken both semesters at the middle school level only. In addition, they have a 45-minute intervention/enrichment period four days a week for reteaching and retesting.

Figure 5.1   Teachers' Schedules: 1st Grade

	Kruse	Miller
8:20-8:30	Homeroom	Homeroom
8:30-9:10	PE (M, W) Music (T, Th) Library skills (F)	PE (T, Th) Music (M, W) Library skills (F)
9:10-9:50	Core literacy reading	Core literacy reading
9:50-10:30	Literacy groups guided reading *Regrouping with Special Ed and Title I teachers*	Literacy groups guided reading *Regrouping with Special Ed and Title I teachers*
10:30-11:10	Core literacy writing/ELA	Core literacy writing/ELA
11:10-11:50	Core math (M/T) Common planning time (W–F)	Core math (M/T) Common planning time (W–F)
11:50-12:10	Recess	Recess
12:10-12:40	Lunch	Lunch
12:45-1:25	Art, Spanish, science, or social studies (varies by day of week)	Art, Spanish, science, or social studies (varies by day of week)
1:25-2:05	Core math	Core math
2:05-2:25	Recess	Recess
2:25-2:45	Core math	Core math
2:45-3:20	Literacy groups/skills *Regrouping with Special Ed and Title I teachers*	Literacy groups/skills *Regrouping with Special Ed and Title I teachers*
3:20-3:25	Dismissal	Dismissal

Source: © 2015 East Union Elementary School, Afton, IA. Used by permission.

Coordinating individual teacher schedules helps, too. At Solon High School in Solon, Iowa, teachers decide individually when they will offer retakes on assessments, but they work together on a buildingwide reassessment schedule. The schedule shows which days and times each teacher offers reassessment. It is shared with all parents and students and is also available on the school's website. Here's an excerpt from the school's reassessment schedule:

Solon High School's Reassessment Schedule for All Teachers

4 x 4 block schedule with daily seminar time for review or reassessment.

	Edwards	Cannon	Smith
Before school	8:00–8:15	7:40–8:00	By appt.
Seminar A	11:16–11:46	By appt.	11:16–11:48 Tuesday-Friday
Seminar B	11:49–12:19	11:46–12:19	By appt.
After school	3:15–4:00		3:15–4:00
PREP block (not open)	4th block	1st block	4th block
Other	By appt.		Click here to sign up with Mr. Smith
Reassessment window	One week before the end of the quarter	End of quarter	Ends one week before the end of the quarter

Source: Solon High School, Solon, IA. Used by permission.

In addition, on the Solon High School web page there is a "High School Assignments" link. The teachers call it the *big board*—it lists major tests and due dates for projects for all teachers by week. Here is an excerpt from the big board:

	Mon 9/8	Tues 9/9	Wed 9/10	Thur 9/11	Fri 9/12
Beck			Quiz S1, S3	Lab report due	ESE Target tests
Erickson		• Advanced Psych • Attribute and prejudice quiz		• Intro Psych • Information processing quiz	

Source: Solon High School, Solon, IA. Used by permission.

Strategic Use of Personnel

Standards-based grading requires additional teacher time. Support personnel may work directly with students, assist teachers in planning, or free teachers for collaborative work.

At East Union High School, in Afton, Iowa, a success coordinator provides Response to Intervention (RTI) for academic and behavioral support. Teachers, parents, or administrators may refer students to the success coordinator. The success coordinator may pull students who aren't working well in class and design interventions specific to their needs. A full-time paraprofessional is also available in the library for students who need individual help during their intervention period. In many schools, RTI staff, paraprofessionals, or teacher aides provide reteaching for groups of students or help teachers to track nonacademic behaviors.

Teachers need time to learn how to unpack standards, how to better check for understanding, and how to successfully target reteaching. Instructional coaches, department heads, or teacher leaders can lessen the workload for teachers and provide them with much needed tools and training. In the Des Moines School District, curriculum coordinators work with small groups of teacher leaders to develop exemplars of formative assessments.

Parkway School District, a large district in Chesterfield, Missouri, has a comprehensive program of support personnel. Each building has a full-time instructional coach who facilitates data meetings, provides building- and district-level professional development, and works with grade-level teams to unpack units of instruction. The district also has 12 math facilitators for 18 elementary buildings. Similar to the instructional coaches, the district also provides support in the areas of data analysis and math instruction preparation to teams in their buildings. As a support to parents in the district, the math facilitators also develop "family letters" for each unit of the K–5 mathematics curriculum. These letters provide families with an overview of the mathematics in their student's current unit as well as suggestions for how to assist at home.

Released time for in-service, individualized support, or to allow teachers to work with students is extremely important. Many schools use early release days or support personnel to cover teachers' classes to allow for that time. At East Union Elementary School in Afton, Iowa, a master teacher and mentor teachers work with classroom teachers. Once a week, two substitutes are hired to release teachers for collaboration.

Other Schoolwide Practices

Schools that have implemented standards-based grading have learned that schoolwide policies help reflect the grading philosophy of the school, promote consistency, and protect teachers from criticism from parents. Many schools require common summative assessments for all sections of a course, and a mandatory retake policy for summative scores below a certain score. Another common practice is to give cumulative exams once a month that may replace formative tests. Many teachers believe this cumulative exam reflects deeper learning and is preferable to arranging retakes.

Student success policies make it harder for students to fail and provide incentives for higher achievement. Federal Way School District in Federal Way, Washington, has an academic acceleration policy that auto-enrolls students in advanced credit classes if they are qualified.

Other schools have open advanced placement and honors classes and allow students to self-select. At East Union Secondary School in Afton, Iowa, students who have shown competency may be accelerated to the next grade for specific subjects. For instance, a 6th grader may be taking 7th grade math or may remain in 6th grade math with differentiations. At the high school level, if students can demonstrate proficiency on the common summative assessments, they may earn credit for the course.

On the flip side, at East Union Secondary School, *F*s are not given for course grades. The lowest grade for credit is a *D* (a 70 percent average). Students who do not receive a minimum score of 70 percent on all summative assignments will receive an Incomplete (I) for the course and must retake the assessments they did not pass. Students must either retake the course or retake the assessments to achieve a passing grade. In order to help students change their incomplete grade, students can arrange to meet with teachers or the success coordinator at the end of the semester. The administration also arranges for school to be open an additional week in the summer to assist students in completing assessments. Some students will work the following semester to change incomplete grades. Incomplete grades are becoming increasingly popular at the secondary level in schools that have implemented standards-based grading.

Many schools have created separate reporting systems for behaviors that were previously part of the grade. At North Middle School in Rapid City, South Dakota, *Learner Responsibilities* are reported separately on the report card. Students are ranked from *1* to *4* in three areas—Independent Practice (Homework), Participation and Collaboration, and Classroom Expectations. A complete rubric is in the Appendix (p. 117).

Des Moines School District in Des Moines, Iowa, uses an Employability Rubric to report nonacademic behaviors on the report card. Students are rated from *0* to *4* on qualities of participation, work completion, behavior, working with peers, and working with others. The complete rubric is found in the Appendix (p. 118–119).

Implementing Standards-Based Grading in the Community: Lessons Learned

Successfully implementing standards-based grading at the school or district level can be tricky business. It's a big change—a change the community often has a hard time understanding and accepting. In the communities that were successful in schoolwide or districtwide grading reform, seeds were planted, early adopters were experimenting, and waters were tested *before* the big plunge into the reform process. Here is advice based on lessons learned from other educators.

1. Start small. In many schools, early adopters pilot standards-based grading, sometimes by grade level, department, team, or alone. Forrest Clark started standards-based grading as a lone math teacher at Nisqually Middle School in Lacey, Washington. Within a few years, he had convinced other middle school math teachers to join him and now all secondary math and science teachers in the district use standards-based grading. Many districts implement standards-based grading at the elementary level first, often starting in the primary grades with just a few teachers.

East Union Secondary School in Afton, Iowa, went a different direction and started by implementing 7–10 common summative assessments in each course, with a weighting of 70 percent for summative assessments. Teachers were allowed to use 30 percent of the grade for homework, participation, and class work. Eventually, the school omitted the 30 percent option and now base 100 percent of the grade on summative assessments.

When the Des Moines Public School District in Des Moines, Iowa, implemented standards-based grading, it started with grades 6 to 8 one year and the following year implemented it with 9th graders. The next step is to use it in both 9th and 10th grades, thus following the first group of 9th graders through high school. With this method, upperclassmen are not suddenly pushed into the standards-based system, and students entering 9th grade will experience standards-based grading for all four years.

2. Let it grow. Most successful school leaders realize that support among teachers needs to grow slowly. They understand it is important to respect teachers' view of grades as their power and their right. As one administrator said, "Teachers need time to grieve the loss of what they thought was right." Given time and the chance to watch early adopters, most other teachers come to see the benefits. Many districts take five to six years to get teachers on board. They wait until a critical mass of teachers are ready before phasing in mandatory changes, and even then, they give teachers plenty of notice.

In Solon, Iowa, after early adopters piloted standards-based grading, they surveyed other teachers. "Where are you on the continuum?" they asked. "Are you ready to implement standards-based grading, do you need more training, or are you not ready?" Based on the survey results, standards-based grading was phased in over a two-year period, allowing additional time, in-service training, and piloting. The next step was that each teacher was required to use standards-based grading in one course. The timeline is shown in Figure 5.2 (p. 94).

3. Include all stakeholders. Schools often begin with a committee who reads the research about standards-based grading, but eventually all stakeholders need to be familiar with at least an abbreviated version of it. Focused shared learning is the foundation of all the other steps. Solon teachers and administrators spent a year reading about the topic from the experts (Guskey, 2006; O'Connor, 2009; Reeves, 2008). Their School Improvement Advisory Committee—community members, PTA representatives, other parents, and school board members—also read materials from the experts.

Figure 5.2   Standards-Based Grading Implementation Plan

2010–2011:	Core group of early adopters (8–10 high school teachers, 2–3 middle school teachers)
2011–2012:	District PD—Reading the work of experts on standards-based grading
	School Improvement Advisory Committee—also reading the work of experts on standards-based grading. The committee is comprised of community members, parents, and the school board.
	Survey of 100 high school students in pilot classrooms
	Survey of teachers—where are you on the continuum?
2012–2013:	All middle school and high school teachers would implement standards-based grading in at least one class by the beginning of 4th quarter.
2013–2014:	All middle school and high school teachers would implement standards-based grading in all classes at the beginning of the school year.

Source: Matt Townsley, Solon School District, Solon, IA. Adapted by permission.

Forest Grove High School in Forest Grove, Oregon, started with a two-day retreat for school improvement that included representatives from all stakeholders—department chairs, building site council parent representatives, the local school committee, the entire school administrative team, and a district office representative. They looked at student data and identified growth areas.

4. Create a belief statement or guiding principles. After focused shared learning comes a shared vision or a set of agreed-upon principles. In successful implementations, stakeholders work together to create a belief statement, statement of guiding principles, or shared vision. In Rock Quarry Middle School in Tuscaloosa, Alabama, teachers spent two years reading and discussing changes that were needed in their grading practices. As a result, they created a grading manifesto that outlined what they believed about grades. On the last day of school all the teachers signed the manifesto. An excerpt follows; the complete manifesto is in the Appendix (p. 107).

Rock Quarry Middle School Grading Manifesto (Excerpt)

At the end of three years (2015–2016), *all* teachers at Rock Quarry Middle School will *fully* implement *exemplary* standards-based grading practices. We commit collectively and individually to improving our professional practice in the areas described below.

• We believe that all grading practices should reflect student achievement only.

We therefore commit to the following:

→ "Extra credit" or bonus points will be awarded **only** when there is evidence additional work resulted in a higher level of academic achievement.

• We believe that behaviors that impede learning should be addressed directly *and kept separate* from academic grades.

We therefore commit to the following:

→ Academic dishonesty (cheating) will be addressed as a *disciplinary* concern. Students who are found to have engaged in academic dishonesty will be required to provide evidence of their actual level of learning.

Source: © 2015 Rock Quarry Middle School, Tuscaloosa, AL. Adapted by permission.

The faculty at Clear Creek Amana Middle School in Tiffin, Iowa, decided on their grading principles. The complete guidelines appear in the Appendix (p. 109).

Clear Creek Amana Middle School
Guidelines for Grading (Excerpt)

Grading principles:

↘ Grades will be based on what the students are able to show they have learned. Therefore, extra credit will not be given at any time.

↘ Retakes and revisions of assessments are allowed.

↘ Students are expected to complete all assigned work.

↘ There will be times when students are expected to do practice work outside of the school day.

Source: © 2015 Clear Creek Amana Middle School, Tiffin, IA. Adapted by permission.

5. Have a comprehensive communication plan. Statements of beliefs or principles serve as the foundation of a comprehensive communication plan. *How* you communicate the message of standards-based grading can yield a smooth, rocky, or failed implementation. The general advice is communicate early, often, and both before and after implementation. Communicate frequently in a variety of formats—websites, fliers at school buildings, letters home, presentations, and face-to-face meetings. Rock Quarry Middle School in Tuscaloosa, Alabama, conducts monthly parent workshops about their standards-based policy. If needed, communicate in more than one language. A successful communication plan includes the following steps:

Appoint a go-to person. A designated contact person at the school or district level is essential. Someone has to run interference. The person's name appears on all communication about standards-based grading. They handle media inquiries, make videos, present to PTA presidents, speak at PTA meetings, and meet with parents individually as needed. In most cases, the contact person is a principal or central office administrator.

Make your website a teaching tool. The school or district website is probably the most important communication tool for parents, the community, and the media. Information must be easy to find with lots of shortcuts to specific information. Parkway School District's website (www.parkwayschools.net) has links to the Common Core State Standards, sample items for new assessments, and standards-based grading book lists, along with summaries of research, teacher blogs, and expert videos by Thomas Guskey, Ken O'Connor, and Rick Wormeli. The Solon Community School District's website (www.solon.k12.ia.us) includes grading guidelines, frequently asked questions, and explanatory videos. Both districts have posted videotaped presentations made for parents on their website. The websites of the Minnetonka District in Minnetonka, Minnesota (www.minnetonka.k12.mn.us) and the Poynette District in Poynette, Wisconsin (www.poynette.k12.wi.us) are also excellent models.

Structure the message to parents. Begin the conversation with parents by focusing on school improvement, *not grading*. Parents are most concerned about the benefits to *their children*—not the features of the system. Use *sound bites* (just like politicians do) to reinforce the most critical ideas in a simple way, such as:

The changes we propose for our students' learning

- are research based,
- are about improving student achievement, and
- will better prepare our students for college and careers.

As a result of our goals, it makes sense that we would change these things about grading.

North Thurston School District in Lacey, Washington, sent a detailed letter and FAQs to all elementary parents. See the Appendix (p. 114) for a copy.

Unfortunately, our message is embedded in language, so we must choose language carefully. We need look no further than the Common Core initiative to see that. Opposition to the Common Core initiative has perverted the image to the point that many schools no longer refer to their standards as Common Core standards. In some communities, schools no longer use the Common Core standards as their rationale for standards-based grading—there's just too much baggage associated with the movement. In fact, in some communities, even the term *standards-based grading* has become negative and schools have instead named their initiatives Grading for Learning, Learner-Focused Grading, or Learner-Centered Assessment and Reporting.

One of the best ways to convince parents that your school needs to change the grading policy is to clearly articulate how the current system is broken. In the Des Moines School District, administrators did that by showing data correlating student grades with ACT scores. Many students with high grades had dismally low ACT and state assessment scores. Other districts show the lack of correlation between student grades and their state standardized test scores. (In one district, students who received *B*s in their math classes ranked from "not proficient" to "exceeds proficiency" on the state math test.)

Most parents focus on getting their child *into* college, so sharing the data about the number of students who *don't graduate* is sobering. This is the "pay me now, pay me later" argument. As one principal said, "We want parents to understand that our school is a safe place to fail—not like work where you get fired, and not like college where it costs the family more money for the student to repeat a class. When do you want to find out your child doesn't know biology? Now or at the University of Iowa?"

When we remove nonacademic behaviors from the grade, the discussion of how we teach responsibility is particularly troublesome for parents. As one administrator said, "Most of our discussions with parents are about whether grades are compensation or communication." We do not want to imply that behaviors are not important—quite the opposite. Our message must be that behaviors are so important they should not be comingled with the academic grade. A few sound bites may help us sell this aspect of standards-based grading to parents:

- Soft skills matter—they are so important we must report them separately and not mask them in the other grade.
- Our current system of grading does not support and value nonacademic skills.
- With our current grading system, if we want to value nonacademic skills, the only way is to use the grade—which can distort the achievement grade and hide the behavior grade.

When we remove nonacademic behaviors from the grade, they have to go somewhere. We have to be able to show parents a system for reporting nonacademic behaviors similar to the rubrics from Rapid City, South Dakota, and the Des Moines Public Schools Citizenship and Employability Skills Rubric (found in the Appendix on p. 118). Once you show parents that such a system actually gives them a clearer and more detailed picture of behaviors, they see the advantage.

6. Make students and teachers your allies. When standards-based grading is well designed and fairly and consistently implemented in a school, students see that they are more in control of their learning and that the new grading system is to their benefit. They can serve as powerful salespeople to parents and to the community.

Many school districts in the early stages of implementation have their students explain the standards-based grading system to their parents during student-led conferences. This process allows parents to ask questions through their child with the teacher present. In the Rock Island–Milan School District in Rock Island, Illinois, elementary students explain learning targets and their new report card to their parents for homework. Here is an excerpt from that assignment:

Teaching about the new report card

Today in school we learned about the new Standards-Based Report Card (show report card).
- It is more detailed than the previous report card.
- It lists the Common Core State Standards that I will be assessed on in math and language arts.
- Not every standard will be assessed every quarter.

Here are some helpful hints for questions your parents may have:
- If they ask, "Why are you getting a new report card?"
- You can say, "The new report card is a clearer picture of what I am able to do according to the standards and where I may need extra help."
- If they ask, "What does N/A mean?"
- You can say, "Not every standard will be assessed each quarter. This is something I will learn in the future."
- You can also write down questions from your parent so your teacher can answer them.

QUESTIONS: _____

_____

_____

_____

Source: Rock Island–Milan School District, Rock Island, IL. Adapted by permission.

Schools in Solon, Iowa, surveyed 100 high school students from pilot classrooms that had used standards-based grading and made that feedback available to parents. Then they had high school teachers and student panels present at parent and school board meetings. Here are some sample student responses from the survey:

- "I like that we can retake things until we understand them because sometimes it takes a while with me for things to click. I also like that it makes you actually learn stuff in order to get a good grade in the class."
- "I like that as a student you have more control over your grade."
- "I like that your grade reflects what you know instead of how many assignments you completed."

Cautionary Tales

The good news is that teachers who are enthusiastic about standards-based grading will sell it to parents and the community. As one administrator said, "Parents trust teachers more than they trust administrators." That's why it is important for schools to take their time and make sure most teachers have embraced the change before a full implementation is planned. Teachers who are reluctant to adopt new methods can be encouraged by other teachers they respect. A few nay-sayers may have little effect, but too many unsupportive teachers can poison the well. That's the bad news. As one principal said, "When teachers are unhappy, parents are unhappy, and the media throws rocks."

This brings us to the cautionary tales of schools that have had a bumpy road in grading reform. The standards-based grading movement is happening all over the country, but not without a few casualties. Just as we learned lessons from what some schools did right, we can also learn lessons from school districts that have struggled to change grading practices. Some have given up and others have been temporarily derailed, but many of these districts will succeed in the future. School boards change, school administrators change, and neighboring school districts influence reform.

No one wants to be the poster child for failed reform. Therefore, these cautionary tales will not mention school districts by name or state, but will merely tell their stories. Suffice it to say that the stories come from all regions of the country and share many similarities. Here are some typical newspaper headlines:

- "Superintendent rolls back standards-based grading used at Riverdale schools"
- "School district revises rules for controversial grading system"
- "New school grade system yanked for this year"
- "Lakeside School District's test-centered grading policy protested"

Here are some missteps that have caused school districts headaches in the process of implementing standards-based grading.

Often failed efforts are a result of "all the parts without the heart." When schools attempt to implement piecemeal policies without the foundation of shared vision, mission, or belief statements, the changes seem arbitrary and without context. The big picture and rationale is missing. When stakeholders (including teachers and parents) don't know why teachers are allowing retakes, no longer giving zeroes, or not counting homework in the grade, emotions run high and the perception is "change for the sake of change" or "you are just making school easier."

Without the shared vision to guide practice, schools often end up with a bastardization of the standards-based grading concept. Schools that neglect to explain to students that homework is important practice for assessments have failed to communicate the concept of formative assessment. Schools that allow unlimited retakes with no proof of remediation have misunderstood the concept. Teachers who are overwhelmed with retakes have failed to connect that problem to feedback and differentiation.

Many school districts that have struggled to implement standards-based grading have suffered from an approach that was too radical—too top-down, too fast, too much at once.

When implementation is top-down with no teacher buy-in, there's often a limited understanding of the changes and no commitment to the mission. Teachers notoriously find ways around policies they had nothing to do with creating. And building principals, being very busy people, may struggle to monitor, much less control, teacher inconsistencies in implementation.

When implementation is too fast, parents may not understand or care that a committee has been studying the changes for years. Parents today feel entitled to a role in what they view as a democratic school system. They expect to be consulted and involved as major changes are proposed. When the community perceives there has been no pilot, and when it appears there is no phase-in stage, they may feel the reform has been ill conceived. If parents say it is a "surprise," groundwork was obviously not laid and communication was lacking.

When implementation is too fast, teachers often do not receive enough professional development or support to do the time-consuming work needed to make the changes. When teachers are told to "just do it," what happens is often "all the parts without the heart"—misapplied practices and a lot of resentment that flows from teacher to student to parent. To illustrate, here's an excerpt from a local newspaper article with the headline "New school grade system yanked for this year":

> Changes to the way county students' grades are calculated that were rolled out in August have been put on hold because of parent and teacher complaints.
>
> "We're stepping back; we're going to take a breath," the school superintendent said Thursday, in her decision late last week to

pull the plug on the grading system changes until next school year.

Elementary schools now will delay their switch to "standards referenced grading" until next August. Principals and teachers at each middle and high school will decide whether to return to the grade calculation system they used last school year or stick with new countywide guidelines.

"I just decided that, try as we may, we didn't have everyone at a good level of understanding," the superintendent said. "I recognized not enough parents had enough time to understand (the new grading system) and some teachers weren't comfortable." (Trible, 2012)

Although piecemeal policy implementation has its issues, so does the opposite. Many schools have had rocky implementations because they tried to do too much at once. That's why many schools start with a department, a grade level, or a school level. For instance, maybe the district can implement the standards-based practices, but still use percentage and letter grades. Maybe implementing standards-based practices *and* translating a 1–100 scale into a *0–4* scale *and* changing the report card all at once is a bit too much. When too much organizational change happens too fast, it is disorienting and people get nervous.

Media as Friend or Foe

As any school administrator or board member knows, the media can be your friend. They can help get the word out about important and positive things happening in your schools. Savvy district leaders seek out pro-education reporters and invite them to parent meetings and community forums. As a result, reporters talk to state colleges and employers about what is needed for students to be college and career ready and then write press releases or articles for the newspaper.

Sometimes it seems that all is well until the media gets involved. A simple axiom here is that if teachers and administrators are happy, the media storm can usually be weathered. But— Angry Teachers + Angry Parents + Media = Trouble. Unfortunately, conflict in general makes good press—the more heated the better ("when it bleeds, it leads"). Overworked, persecuted teachers make great press. Here are a few quotes from newspaper articles:

- "Teachers are complaining, 'We have so much extra grading to do now, it's just too much!'"
- "In a recent letter to the school board, teachers singled out grading changes, among other new initiatives, they say added stress, swelled workload, and hurt morale."

Organized grassroots movements by parents also make great press. Dramatic statements like "Standards-based grading is hurting our kids, dumbing down the curriculum, ruining values" make great press. There is a growing educational activism among parents, and social media makes it easy to vent concerns and find other like-minded parents. Never underestimate the ability of a small group of people to make a lot of noise, especially once they get a website (such as www.stopsbg.com), a Facebook page, or a Twitter account.

The good news is that even school districts with very vocal opposition have been able to successfully implement standards-based grading. The secret to success is that teachers and administrators understand their job is never done and that standards-based grading is always a "work in progress." They continue to address parent and community concerns and compromise when needed, but remain focused on the students. When teachers and administrators believe in the rightness of what they are doing, they continue to refine programs and procedures and continue to inspire new teachers, administrators, and board members to come on board. They tirelessly collect data on the benefit of standards-based grading to student learning, graduation rates, and college success. They continue to share positive evidence with parents and the community. And eventually the results are undeniable.

Conclusion

A revolution in education is happening. Teachers and administrators are reexamining grading practices and thinking outside the box like never before. Those who have successfully implemented standards-based grading are spreading the word to others at state and national conferences. They will tell you what you already know—that change is never easy and old habits and outdated beliefs die hard. But they will also tell remarkable stories of student success and teacher revitalization. They will tell you to stay the course and keep the faith. It is an exciting journey.

Afterword

Long before standards-based grading came along, teachers knew that under the right conditions more students could succeed. They were questioning and experimenting: "What if we gave them more time? What if we changed the schedule? What if we changed how we teach? What if we demanded more from them?" But as they tried to implement their ideas, the existing system hemmed them in. It even restricted their thinking: "Great idea, but, the student has to stay in the 2nd grade, the period is 50 minutes long, and the school year is over in June."

The principles of standards-based grading have helped us break out of those barriers and caused us to rethink the most ingrained practices and organizational structures of schooling. The standards-based grading approach is the synthesis of years of research and instinctive wisdom about effective teaching and learning. It pulls it all together in a system that just makes sense.

Does implementing standards-based grading require us to "subvert the dominant paradigm"? Most definitely. Will it be easy? Probably not. Is it worth it? Without a doubt. It is an investment in the future success of our students. This is why we teach.

• • •

Appendix

Grading Manifesto

At the end of three years (2015–2016), *all* teachers at Rock Quarry Middle School will *fully* implement *exemplary* standards-based grading practices. We commit collectively and individually to improving our professional practice in the areas described below.

⭷ We believe that all grading practices should reflect student achievement only.
We therefore commit to the following:

➔ Absences will be tracked and reported as required by policy. However, all attendance issues will be kept separate from grade determination.

➔ To the greatest degree possible, student behaviors (including, but not limited to, effort, participation, adherence to class rules) will be excluded as a factor in grade calculation.

➔ "Extra credit" or bonus points will be awarded only when there is evidence that additional work has resulted in a higher level of academic achievement.

➔ When evidence of learning is missing, we will work to obtain evidence of that student's real achievement.

⇘ We believe that behaviors that impede learning should be addressed directly *and kept separate* from academic grades.

We therefore commit to the following:

→ Academic dishonesty (cheating) will be addressed as a *disciplinary* concern. Students who are found to have engaged in academic dishonesty will be required to provide evidence of their actual level of learning.

→ To the greatest degree possible, student *compliance* (completing homework, submitting assignments on time, etc.) will be addressed outside the context of academic grades.

⇘ We believe that students can (and should) achieve high academic proficiency if the performance goals are clear and well aligned with instructional activities.

We therefore commit to the following:

→ We will provide clear descriptions of achievement expectations for each activity, lesson, and unit of study. Grades will be based on each individual student's mastery of these learning objectives.

→ Each student's performance will be compared to pre-set standards and expectations.

⇘ We believe that assessment is most effective if done *with* students rather than *to* students.

We therefore commit to the following:

→ We will include students in the assessment/grading process. They can—and will—play key roles in examining and describing their own academic achievement under the guidance of the teacher.

→ We will make collaborative learning a priority. However, evidence of learning will be documented *individually*.

Guidelines for Grading

Grading Mission. At Clear Creek Amana Middle School, we strive to ensure that the letter grade that a student achieves is based on true assessments and that the grade represents learning and student understanding of the standards.

Grading Principles

- Differentiation of instruction is essential in order for students to grow and progress.
- We value our students' attendance, behavior, cooperation, motivation, and positive attitude.
- Grades will be based on what the students are able to show they have learned. Therefore, extra credit will not be given at any time.
- Retakes and revisions of assessments are allowed.
- Students will be allowed multiple opportunities to demonstrate proficiency in various ways. When proficiency is demonstrated, students will be given the opportunity to extend their learning.
- Students are expected to complete all assigned work.
- There will be times when students are expected to do practice work outside of the school day.
- Independent practice will be meaningful, purposeful, of high quality, and aligned with learning goals.
- Teachers will determine proficiency by considering multiple points of data emphasizing the most recent data and provide evidence to support their determination.
- Students will have multiple opportunities for practice before the learning goals are assessed for a proficiency score.

Powerschool Grade Book Entry

When entering academic grades into Powerschool, teachers will use the rubric outlined below.

Grading Rubric

Statement	Rubric Number	Percentage	Grade	Comment
Exceeds	4	100%	A	• I can complete the task without help. • I can explain how to do the task in my own words. • I can help someone who is struggling with the task. • I can explain how it applies to my life.
Secure	3.5	87.5%	B	• I can complete the task without help. • I can show that I understand. • I can find my own mistakes.
Developing	3	75%	C	• I can complete the task with help or an example in front of me. • I may still make a few mistakes. • I can find my mistakes with help from someone.
Beginning	2	50%	F Not Acceptable	• I can follow the task while someone explains it to me. • I cannot figure out what I am doing wrong. • I cannot figure out how to start.

Grading Terms

Some of the terms you may hear students or teachers talk about at our middle school are defined below.

Learning goals are the foundation for all of our lessons and assessments. The learning goals should match our Iowa Core Standards. Example learning goal from social studies: The students will understand how physical processes and human actions modify the environment and how the environment affects humans.

Success criteria should be observable and/or measurable. Success criteria are what the students are asked to show their ability to do. Normally success criteria are written using "I can" statements. Example success criteria from social studies: I can describe how the physical features of Australia impact population density.

A *rubric* is a scoring tool that lists the criteria for a piece of work. For example, a rubric for an essay might tell students that their work will be judged on purpose, organization, details, voice, and mechanics. A good rubric also describes levels of quality for each of the criteria, usually on a point scale.

Differentiated instruction is what teachers do to meet the needs of ALL learners.

Middle School Parent Letter About Grading Policy

Dear Parent/Guardian,

This grading policy is designed to accurately communicate your student's mastery of math content, separate from effort, participation, or numbers of papers turned in. We believe this provides an accurate picture of your student's academic progress and potential for moving on to algebra.

1. Math grades will be based upon demonstrated mastery of state math standards (Performance Expectations). **100 percent** of the grade is based upon assessment scores. Grades will **NOT** include points for effort, HOMEWORK, participation, or extra credit.

2. Homework completion will be tracked, but will **NOT** count toward the grade.

3. Tests will be organized by standard and each standard will receive a separate score.

4. Students need test scores of **80 percent or higher** on a standard to demonstrate mastery.

5. Students scoring below 80 percent on any standard(s) will take an in-class retest on those standard(s) only. Students scoring above 80 percent can choose to take an optional retest.

6. Students still scoring below 80 percent after the in-class retest are allowed additional retests before or after school at the teacher's discretion. Students **MUST** complete test corrections or at least 75 percent of their homework or retest practice work in order to retest.

7. At the end of each grading period (quarter), there will be a Final Exam that addresses all standards taught during that quarter. Final Exams will be organized and scored by standard and will count as a retest. These scores will replace any lower grade book entries. **FINAL EXAM SCORES CAN ONLY RAISE PREVIOUS GRADE BOOK ENTRIES. NO ENTRIES ALREADY IN THE GRADE BOOK WILL BE LOWERED.**

8. End of course letter grades will be determined by averaging the scores in the grade book. However, when the average is skewed by outlier scores, the median may be used to determine the final letter grade.

   Please discuss these procedures with your student and make sure he or she understands that each student is expected to master EACH individual concept at 80 percent, and that there will be an opportunity for review and extra help prior to retesting. If you have any additional questions, please contact me at jsmith@jones.k12.xx.xx or 111-2222.

Sincerely,

J. Smith
8th Grade Math Teacher

Source: Used by permission of Nisqually Middle School, Lacey, Washington.

Elementary Parent Letter About a Common Report Card

Dear Parents and Guardians,

Our school district will be using a common report card in all classrooms this year. This report card is different from the traditional report cards in that students will be assessed against grade-level standards and expectations after instruction and practice has been given. Here is what each number means:

4 = Exceeds grade-level standards
- **Consistently** meets requirements for **exceptional** work
- Demonstrates **high** level of knowledge and understanding

3 = Meets grade-level standards
- **Consistently** meets requirements for **proficient** work
- Demonstrates **acceptable** level of knowledge and understanding

2 = Approaching grade-level standards
- Meets some requirements for proficient work
- Demonstrates some knowledge and understanding

1 = Significantly below standards
- Meets few requirements for proficient work
- Demonstrates little knowledge and understanding

Please note that even if the student gets all the answers correct, he or she still may receive a 3 in a specific area. Until that student shows **exceptional** work and understanding **consistently**, we will not give out a 4.

If your student received a 2 or a 1 in any category, please review this area at home. It is essential that the student practices at home in order to truly internalize and retain the information.

Please let us know if you have any other questions. Our goal is to give you a more accurate and informative understanding of how your student is doing in school.

Thank you for all the home support!

Sincerely,
Elementary Principal

Elementary School Grading FAQs
What is the purpose of the standards-based report card?

The purpose of this report card is to give a clear picture of the child's achievement on key academic targets. These targets, reflecting the learning standards of the State of Washington, have been identified as particularly important for students' success as they continue through school.

How is this report card different from previous report cards?

In the past, letter grades included evidence from class work, homework, class participation, and sometimes effort. Grades on the standards-based report card are based on key assignments, tests, observations, and individual conferences, all of which are completed *after instruction*. Most assignments and much of the work done by students *in the process of learning new material* are not reflected in report card grades. Instead, this "practice" work will be used to help students and teachers know what to focus on in the learning.

Does the report card give information about behavior, effort, and study skills?

Yes. Information on behavior, effort, and study skills is reported separately from the academic information in a section called "Characteristics of Successful Learners." There is also a place for teacher comments.

What is the advantage of the standards-based report card for a parent?

You learn more about how your child is actually achieving in school. Clearer reporting allows better communication among teachers, parents, and students. This helps teachers, students, and parents focus on skill development and standards of proficiency rather than on grades. You will experience more consistency in the marking processes across the district.

My child usually gets excellent marks (*As* or the equivalent of *As*). Does this mean my child will get all 4s on the new report card?

No. A 4 on the new card does not equal an *A*. The scores (4, 3, 2, or 1) are based on whether a child's performances on key assignments typically exceed standards, meet standards, fall somewhat below standards, or fall significantly below standards. In prior reporting an *A* may have meant that a child met all the standards for the test or assignment; in the new report card, this would be represented by a 3. A 4 on the new report card means that a student is regularly able to demonstrate a level of skill and understanding beyond the proficiency standard for his or her grade level.

Source: © 2015 North Thurston Public Schools, Lacey, Washington. Adapted by permission.

Learner Responsibilities of North Middle School Students

	4 – Consistently Exceeds Expectations	3 – Consistently Meets Expectations	2 – Inconsistently Meets Expectations	1 – Does Not Meet Expectations
Independent Practice -Homework	Consistently attempts the problems and provides evidence of mathematical thinking.	Usually attempts the problems and provides evidence of mathematical thinking.	Sometimes attempts the problems and provides some evidence of mathematical thinking.	Rarely attempts the problems or provides evidence of mathematical thinking.
Participates in Learning -Collaboration	Consistently shares information or ideas when participating in discussion or groups. Regularly uses teamwork and leadership skills to help and encourage others.	Usually shares information or ideas when participating in discussions or groups. Usually uses teamwork and leadership skills to help and encourage others.	Sometimes shares information or ideas when participating in discussion or groups. Sometimes uses teamwork and leadership skills to help and encourage others.	Rarely shares ideas. May refuse to participate. In groups, relies on the work of others. Rarely uses teamwork and leadership skills to help and encourage others.
Follows Classroom Expectations	Consistently follows classroom expectations and routines.	Usually follows classroom expectations and routines.	Sometimes follows classroom expectations and routines.	Rarely follows classroom expectations and routines.

Source: © 2014 Rapid City, SD. Adapted by permission.

Citizenship and Employability Skills Rubric

	Academic Conduct	Work Completion	Working with Other Students	Working with Adults
Exceeding 4	**The student** • Arrives on time, prepared for class every day. • Participates every day, actions drive instruction forward. • Consistently does what's expected and helps others do the same.	**The student** • Completes work as assigned every day. • Routinely submits work on time. • Takes full advantage of retake/redo opportunities and support.	**The student** • Effectively leads a group of students. • Can help resolve most conflicts. • Seeks out different points of view. • Embraces diversity in others.	**The student** • Assumes responsibility for learning by seeking help and asking questions in a timely manner. • Consistently listens and follows suggestions given by adults. • Consistently demonstrates effective communication skills and willingness to work with adults.
Meeting 3	**The student** • Arrives on time, prepared for class consistently. • Participates in class, actions benefit instruction. • Accepts responsibility for actions, rarely requires redirection.	**The student** • Consistently completes work assigned. • Usually submits work on time. • Takes advantage of retake/redo opportunities and support.	**The student** • Effectively communicates with other students. • Does not participate in conflicts. • Accepts different points of view. • Accepts diversity in others.	**The student** • Usually assumes responsibility for learning by seeking help and asking questions when needed. • Usually listens and follows suggestions given by adults. • Usually demonstrates effective communication skills and willingness to work with adults.

	The student	The student	The student	The student
Developing 2	The student • Arrives on time, prepared for class inconsistently. • Participates in class, actions at times distract from instruction. • Usually follows redirection and changes actions.	The student • Inconsistently completes work as assigned. • Inconsistently submits work on time. • Occasionally takes advantage of retake/redo opportunities and support.	The student • Occasionally communicates effectively with other students. • Does not escalate conflicts. • Occasionally accepts different points of view. • Occasionally accepts diversity in others.	The student • Occasionally seeks help and asks questions when needed. • Inconsistently listens and follows suggestions given by adults. • Sometimes demonstrates effective communication skills and willingness to work with adults.
Beginning or Insufficient Progress 1	The student • Rarely brings materials to class, even with teacher coaching. • Rarely participates, comments often distract from instruction. • Does not follow redirection to change actions.	The student • Rarely completes work as assigned. • Rarely submits work on time. • Rarely takes advantage of retake/redo opportunities and support.	The student • Does not communicate effectively with other students. • Escalates conflict. • Does not accept different points of view. • Does not accept diversity in others.	The student • Rarely seeks help and asks questions when needed. • Rarely listens and follows suggestions given by adults. • Rarely demonstrates effective communication skills and willingness to work with adults.
No Evidence 0	Even with help, the student • Does not bring materials. • Does not participate. • Does not follow directions. • Escalates situation when given redirection.	Even with help, the student • Does not complete work as assigned. • Does not submit work on time. • Does not take advantage of retake/redo opportunities and support.	The student • Initiates conflict. Even with help, the student • Does not communicate effectively. • Does not accept different points of view. • Does not accept diversity.	Even with help, the student • Does not seek help and ask questions. • Does not listen and follow suggestions given by adults. • Does not demonstrate effective communication skills or a willingness to work with adults.

* All bullet points are indicators for the level. Not all indicators must be met in order to score a student at a particular level in each category.

Source: Adapted with permission from Des Moines Public Schools.

References

ACT, Inc. (2005). Are high school grades inflated? *Issues in College Readiness.* Author. ERIC: ED510537.

Beecher, M., & Fischer, L. (1999, Spring/Summer). High school courses and scores as predictors of college success. *Journal of College Admissions, 163,* 4–9.

Bonstingl, J. J. (1992). The quality revolution. *Educational Leadership, 50*(3), 4–9.

Brookhart, S. M. (2008). *How to give effective feedback to your students.* Alexandria, VA: ASCD.

Brookhart, S. M. (2011). Starting the conversation about grading. *Educational Leadership, 69*(3), 10–14.

Brooks, J. G., & Dietz, M. E. (2012). The dangers and opportunities of the Common Core. *Educational Leadership, 70*(4), 64–67.

Canady, R. (2010). *School policies and grading practices that increase/decrease the odds for student success.* National Middle School Association's annual conference, Baltimore, MD.

Canady, R. L., & Hotchkiss, P. R. (1989). It's a good score! Just a bad grade. *Phi Delta Kappan, 1*(1), 68–71.

Canter, L. (1976). *Assertive discipline: A take-charge approach for today's educator.* Los Angeles: Lee Canter and Associates.

Canter, L., & Canter, M. (1992). *Assertive discipline: Positive behavior management for today's classroom.* Santa Monica, CA: Lee Canter and Associates.

Chappuis, J. (2009). *Seven strategies of assessment for learning.* Portland, OR: ETS Assessment Training Institute.

Curreton, L.W. (1971). The history of grading practices. *National Council on Measurement in Education, 2*(4), 1–9.

DeLorenzo, R. A., Battino, W. J., Schreiber, R. M., & Gaddy Carrio, B. (2009). *Delivering on the promise: The education revolution.* Bloomington, IN: Solution Tree.

Durm, M. W. (1993, Spring). An *A* is not an *A*: A history of grading. *The Educational Forum, 57,* 1–4.

Dweck, C. (2007). *Mindset: The new psychology of success.* New York: Ballantine.

Education Week. (2013). Diplomas count 2013, executive summary: Making progress and trying again. *Education Week, 32*(34), 1.

Freiberg, H. J. (1999). Beyond behaviorism. In H. J. Freiberg, (Ed.), *Beyond behaviorism: Changing the classroom management paradigm* (pp. 3–20). Needham Heights, MA: Allyn and Bacon.

Friedman, T. L., & Mandelbaum, M. (2012). *That used to be us: How America fell behind in the world it invented and how we can come back.* New York: Picador.

Geiser, S., & Santelices, M. V. (2007). Validity of high-school grades in predicting student success beyond the freshman year: High-school record vs. standardized tests as indicators of four-year college outcomes. *Center for Studies in Higher Education Research and occasional paper series: CSHE.6-07.* Berkeley, CA: University of California, Berkeley.

Glasser, W. (1992). *The quality school: Managing students without coercion.* New York: HarperCollins.

Goodwin, B. (2011). Grade inflation: Killing with kindness? *Educational Leadership, 69*(3), 80–81.

Guskey, T. R. (1996). *Communicating student learning. ASCD yearbook.* Alexandria, VA: ASCD.

Guskey, T. R. (2006). Making high school grades meaningful. *Phi Delta Kappan,* 87(9), 670–675.

Guskey, T. R. (2007). Using assessments to improve teaching *and* learning. In D. Reeves (Ed.), *Ahead of the curve: The power of assessment to transform teaching and learning* (pp. 15–29). Bloomington, IN: Solution Tree.

Guskey, T. R. (2011). Five obstacles to grading reform. *Educational Leadership, 69*(3), 16–21.

Guskey, T. R. (2015). *On your mark: Challenging the conventions of grades and reporting.* Bloomington, IN: Solution Tree.

Guskey, T. R., & Bailey, J. M. (2001). *Developing grading and reporting systems for student learning.* Thousand Oaks, CA: Corwin.

Hanushek, E. A. (2004). *Some simple analytics of school quality* (Working paper 10229). Cambridge, MA: National Bureau of Economic Quality.

Hattie, J. (2009). *Visible learning: A synthesis of over 800 meta-analyses relative to achievement.* New York: Routledge.

Herman, J., & Linn, R. (2014). New assessments, new rigor. *Educational Leadership, 71*(6), 34–37.

Hershberg, T. (2005). Value-added assessment and systemic reform: A response to the challenge of human capital development. *Phi Delta Kappan, 87*(4), 276–283.

Jensen, A. R. (1980). *Bias in mental testing.* New York: Free Press.

Kelly, T. F. (2009). Grade inflation: Sense and nonsense. *Phi Delta Kappan, 90*(9), 696.

Kirschenbaum, H., Simon, S. B., & Napier, R. W. (1971). *Wad-ja-get: The grading game in American education.* New York: Hart.

Kohn, A. (1993). *Punished by rewards: The trouble with gold stars, incentive plans, A's, praise, and other bribes.* New York: Houghton Mifflin.

Kohn, A. (1999). *Punished by rewards: The trouble with gold stars, incentive plans, A's, praise, and other bribes (2nd ed.).* New York: Houghton Mifflin.

Kohn, A. (2002). The dangerous myth of grade inflation. *Chronicle of Higher Education, 49*(11), B7.

Marzano, R. J. (2000). *Transforming classroom grading.* Alexandria, VA: ASCD.

McClellan, B. E. (1999). *Moral education in America: Schools and the shaping of character from colonial times to the present.* New York: Teachers College Press.

Milton, O., Pollio, H. R., & Eison, J. A. (1986). *Making sense of college grades.* San Francisco: Jossey-Bass.

Moss, C. M., & Brookhart, S. M. (2012). *Learning targets: Helping students aim for understanding in today's lesson.* Alexandria, VA: ASCD.

O'Connor, K. (2009). *How to grade for learning K–12 (3rd ed.).* Thousand Oaks, CA: Corwin.

OIRP. (2011). *High school GPA and SAT score effects on graduation rates.* Office of Institutional Research and Policy Studies, March 18.

Oxtoby, D. W. (2007). The rush to take more AP courses hurts students, high schools, and colleges. *Education Digest, 73*(1), 43–46.

Pope, D. C. (2001). *"Doing school": How we are creating a generation of stressed out, materialistic, and miseducated students.* New Haven, CT: Yale University Press.

Reeves, D. (2011). *Elements of grading: A guide to effective practice.* Bloomington, IN: Solution Tree.

Reeves, D. B. (2008). Leading to change/Effective grading practices. *Educational Leadership, 65*(5), 85–87.

Schimmer, T. (2012). *Ten things that matter from assessment to grading.* Toronto, Ontario: Pearson.

Schimmer, T. (2013a). *Infused assessment.* Presented at the Assessment Training Institute, Portland, Oregon, July 8.

Schimmer, T. (2013b). *Accurate grading with a standards-based mindset.* Sound Grading Practices Conference: Leading the change in classroom grading, Portland, Oregon, December 6.

Schmidt, P. (2007, March 9). High-school students aim higher without learning more, federal studies find. *Chronicle of Higher Education, 53*(27), A32.

Seligman, M. (1998). *Learned optimism.* New York: Pocket Books.

Starch, D., & Elliott, E. C. (1912). Reliability of the grading of high school work in English. *School Review,* 20.

Starch, D., & Elliott, E. C. (1913). Reliability of grading work in mathematics. *School Review,* 21.

Stewart, V. (2012). *A world-class education: Learning from international models of excellence and innovation.* Alexandria, VA: ASCD.

Stiggins, R. (2007). Assessment *for* learning: An essential foundation of productive instruction. In D. Reeves (Ed.), *Ahead of the curve: The power of assessment to transform teaching and learning* (pp. 59–78). Bloomington, IN: Solution Tree.

Stiggins, R. J. (2005). *Student-involved assessment for learning.* Upper Saddle River, NJ: Pearson.

Strom, P. S., & Strom, R. D. (2007). Cheating in middle school and high school. *Educational Forum, 71*(2), 104–116.

Stumpf, H., & Stanley, J. C. (2002). Group data on high school grade point average and scores on academic aptitude tests as predictors of institutional graduation rates. *Educational and Psychological Measurement, 62*(6), 1042–1052.

Thayer, V. T. (1965). *Formative ideas in American education from the colonial period to the present.* New York: Dodd, Mead.

Tomlinson, C. (2008). The goals of differentiation. *Educational Leadership, 66*(3), 26–30.

Tomlinson, C. (2014). The bridge between today's lesson and tomorrow's. *Educational Leadership, 71*(6), 10–14.

Tough, P. (2012). *How children succeed: Grit, curiosity, and the hidden power of character.* New York: Houghton Mifflin Harcourt.

Trible, L. (2012). New school grade system yanked for this year. *The Daytona Beach News-Journal,* October 4.

U.S. Department of Education. (2010). *Forest Grove High School (Transformational Model).* Author: Washington, DC. Retrieved from http://www.ed.gov/oese-news/forest-grove.

U.S. Department of Education. (2012a). Science Literacy: Average Scores (Overall). Retrieved from https://nces.ed.gov/surveys/pisa/pisa2012/pisa2012highlights_4a.asp

U.S. Department of Education. (2012b). Mathematics Literacy: Average Scores (Overall). Retrieved from https://nces.ed.gov/surveys/pisa/pisa2012/pisa2012highlights_3a.asp

U.S. Department of Education. (2012c). Reading Literacy: Average Scores (Overall). Retrieved from https://nces.ed.gov/surveys/pisa/pisa2012/pisa2012highlights_5a.asp

Varlas, L. (2013). How we got grading wrong, and what to do about it. *Education Update*, *55*(10), 1, 6–7.

Vatterott, C. (2007). *Becoming a middle level teacher: Student focused teaching of early adolescents.* New York: McGraw-Hill.

Vatterott, C. (2009). *Rethinking homework: Best practices that support diverse needs.* Alexandria, VA: ASCD.

Vatterott, C. (2010). Five hallmarks of good homework. *Educational Leadership, 68*(1), 10–15.

Vatterott, C. (2011). Making homework central to learning. *Educational Leadership, 69*(3), 60–64.

Vatterott, C. (2014). Student-owned homework. *Educational Leadership, 71*(6), 39–42.

Wiggins, G., & McTighe, J. (2005). *Understanding by design* (expanded 2nd edition). Alexandria, VA: ASCD.

Wiliam, D. (2007). Content *then* process: Teacher learning communities in the service of formative assessment. In D. Reeves (Ed.), *Ahead of the curve: The power of assessment to transform teaching and learning* (pp. 182–204). Bloomington, IN: Solution Tree.

Williamson, R., & Johnston, J. H. (1999). Challenging orthodoxy: An emerging agenda for middle level reform. *Middle School Journal, 30*(4), 10–17.

Zirkel, P. A. (2007). Grade inflation: High schools' skeleton in the closet. *Education Week, 26*(29), 40, 30.

Zmuda, A. (2008). Springing into active learning. *Educational Leadership, 66*(3), 38–42.

Index

Note: The letter *f* following a page number denotes a figure.

About the Author

Cathy Vatterott, PhD, is a professor of education at the University of Missouri–St. Louis, and was a middle school and high school teacher and a former middle school principal. She is the author of numerous articles about education and three books, *Academic Success Through Empowering Students* (NMSA), *Becoming a Middle Level Teacher: Student-focused Teaching of Early Adolescents* (McGraw-Hill), and *Rethinking Homework: Best Practices That Support Diverse Needs* (ASCD). Dr. Vatterott is considered a national expert on the topic of K–12 homework and is often interviewed by reporters from the *New York Times, National Public Radio, BBC World News Service*, and *USA Today*, as well as writers from parenting magazines and educational organizations.

Discussions about the grading of homework in her presentatios in the United States and Canada revealed a major disconnect between how grades are typically used in K–12 classrooms and our goal of helping students meet academic standards. These discussions have been the catalyst for her latest research about K–12 standards-based grading. She can be reached at vatterott@umsl.edu or through her website at www.homeworklady.com.

Related ASCD Resources: Assessment and/or Standards

At the time of publication, the following ASCD resources were available (ASCD stock numbers appear in parentheses). For up-to-date information about ASCD resources, go to www.ascd.org. You can search the complete archives of *Educational Leadership* at http://www.ascd.org/el.

Books

Accountability for Learning: How Teachers and School Leaders Can Take Charge by Douglas B. Reeves (#104004)

Classroom Assessment & Grading That Work by Robert J. Marzano (#106006)

The Core Six: Essential Strategies for Achieving Excellence with the Common Core by Harvey F. Silver, R. Thomas Dewing, and Matthew J. Perini (#113007)

Grading and Group Work: How Do I Assess Individual Learning When Students Work Together? (ASCD Arias) by Susan M. Brookhart (#109031)

Grading Smarter, Not Harder: Assessment Strategies That Motivate Kids and Help Them Learn by Myron Dueck (#114003)

The Learning Leader: How to Focus School Improvement for Better Results by Douglas B. Reeves (#105051)

Test Better, Teach Better: The Instructional Role of Assessment by W. James Popham (#102088)

Transformative Assessment by W. James Popham (#108018)

Transformative Assessment in Action: An Inside Look at Applying the Process by W. James Popham (#111008)

What Teachers Really Need to Know About Formative Assessment by Laura Greenstein (#110017)

ASCD EDge Group

Exchange ideas and connect with other educators interested in assessment and grading (Let's Talk Assessment and Grading) or standards (ASCD's Common Core Standards) on the social networking site ASCD EDge™ at http://ascdedge.ascd.org/

THE WHOLE CHILD The Whole Child Initiative helps schools and communities create learning environments that allow students to be healthy, safe, engaged, supported, and challenged. To learn more about other books and resources that relate to the whole child, visit www.wholechildeducation.org.

For more information: send e-mail to member@ascd.org; call 1-800-933-2723 or 703-578-9600, press 2; send a fax to 703-575-5400; or write to Information Services, ASCD, 1703 N. Beauregard St., Alexandria, VA 22311-1714 USA.